GRACE OR WORKS?

GRACE OR WORKS?

By
Oluwakemi O. Ola-Ojo
©2009

*Unless otherwise indicated, all Scripture quotations
are from the King James Version [KJV] of the Holy Bible.*

*Grace or Works?
ISBN 978-0-9557898-5-4*

*Copyright © 2009
by Oluwakemi O. Ola-Ojo*

All rights belong exclusively to Protokos Publishers.

*Published by
Protokos Publishers
P.O. Box 48424
London
SE15 2YL
www.protokospublishers.com
+44 (0)7534831807*

Author's photograph by Hill Stanton

Printed by Lightning Source,
United Kingdom.

*Cover design by www.dmaudiovisuals.com
Printed in the United Kingdom.*

*All rights reserved under International Copyright Law. Contents and/
or cover may not be reproduced in whole or in part in any form without
the express written consent of the Publishers.*

Grace or Works?

Dedication:

To every:
- Parent or person who has experienced or who is experiencing coping with the challenges of a 'prodigal child, sibling, husband, wife, father or mother'.
- Once before prodigal child or person who has retraced his/her steps back home – physical or spiritual.
- One who had once thought that making heaven is by works but who now knows better – it is by grace not of works lest any man should boast.
- One helping others to find their way back to the love of God.

Appreciation

Our God deserves all the praise and worship for this revelation.

I wish to thank Mrs Bolanle Sogunro for editing this book and Kunle Falodun for his wonderful creativity. To all who found time to read and comment on this manuscript, I'd like to say a big thank you.

To the helpful team at Cyber hymnal whose help has made the hymns available on the Internet and to Kingsway Thank you Music, God richly bless you all.

I am most grateful to the Management and staff of DMU Audiovisuals for the unique cover design of this book.. I also appreciate the staff of Protokos Publishers for helping to publish and market my books.

Finally, but not in the least, I am grateful to Sharon Dennis an outstanding friend who found time out of none to type the first manuscript.

Contents

Dedication	v
Appreciation	vi
Background	viii
Preface	x
Chapter 1 The Younger Son	16
Chapter 2 The Elder Son	45
Chapter 3 The Loving Father	65
Chapter 4 Grace or Works?	84
Chapter 5 More Poems to Inspire You	87
• The Dead End	87
• Conquering the Problem	89
• Facing the Past	92
• Sin	94
• I Loved them both Dearly	96
• God's Love like the Sun	97
• The Beauty of the Snow	100
• Summer in the West	103
• Cafeteria.	106
Opportunity to Become a Christian	109
Useful addresses	110
Other books by the Author	114

Grace or Works?

Background

It must have been in 1995 after being gainfully unemployed in England for about three years I came to the end of myself. Coming to England for further studies for me was following many revelations and a confirmation of God's leading and His promise to bless me and use me to bless others in the trip abroad. I was neither on any scholarship nor had I any award so I had to work to pay for my studies. I had no problems securing a job with one degree when I arrived but surprisingly, after securing two more post graduate University degrees, I was faced with failure in job interviews and being told I couldn't have the jobs, I came to the end of myself. I was not on any form of Government benefit as I had come on a student visa and no immediate family of mine was in England to help. Only God knows how I survived those dark years.

For a whole week I locked myself in my flat in London and the only story that appealed to me was the story of the prodigal son recorded in Luke 15:11-32. I read it over and over throughout the week, x-raying my life in the light of the truth of the story. In some ways, my situation was like that of the younger son in a strange land and in a desperate financial crisis. I recalled what life was like back home for me before I came abroad. Though my coming was God-ordained and God-led, in the light of the prevailing severe unending financial crisis, I came to the same conclusion as that of the younger son that I would return home and at least be guaranteed of my three square meals. Speeches were prepared for

Grace or Works?

the various categories of people that I would have to face when I returned home - from my family and friends to my colleagues and employer at work. This write up is the inspiration that the Holy Spirit gave me in the week I locked myself in.

Unlike the prodigal son, I did not come with my family inheritance to seek for adventure; I came based on God's promises. Like the prodigal son, when times became too hard, I remembered what life was like for me at home before coming over and I too decided to go back home since all was no longer going as I had felt revealed to me, thought or planned. Like the prodigal son, I actually prepared my speeches to my parents, family, employer, colleagues and friends. I rehearsed the speeches over and over.

Then a letter arrived for another interview for Thursday. I couldn't be bothered to prepare for this interview but attended to keep my promise to the Personnel Department of that hospital. I had made plans to phone my brother in Lagos and send a message through him to my parents asking them to send me the promised return ticket on Friday.

I was shocked to be told a few minutes after the interview that I was successful and the hospital would want me to start work as soon as possible. Such was the shock that I was in that it took over thirty minutes after leaving the hospital premises before I could say, 'Thank You God!' All I could say for that first thirty minutes or so was, 'I want to go back home' (like in the ET movie), a phrase that still brings tears to my eyes when I remember.

Child of God, don't give up your faith, don't give in to the devil, your miracle is nearer than you could ever imagine. Just re-align your life with Him.

Preface

The tradition at the time of the story of the prodigal son is presumed to be that of the Old Testament where the family wealth especially that of the land and cattle, was to be kept as much as possible within the family.

Such wealth was subject to sharing amongst the male children upon their father's death. The eldest son was meant to have twice the share of others so that he would be able to cater for the other family members e.g. the widowed mother and any unmarried sisters. Whilst the father was alive, the wealth was within his prerogative to do as he wished (Genesis 25:5-6; 27:27-29). If any was poor and sold the land, it was to be returned to its owner in the year of Jubilee (Leviticus 25:23-28).

In a family that had only girls, they were entitled to their father's inheritance on the condition that they married men from their tribe (Joshua 17:3-4). This way, the land eventually remains in the family for inheritance.

Jesus' approach in teaching the people many times was in parables, using the common place events to teach spiritual truths.

Whilst 1 Corinthians 13 has been used to teach " AGAPE LOVE" I believe the parable of the father and his two sons popularly

Grace or Works?

referred to as the parable of the prodigal son is as relevant to us today as it was in the time of Jesus. It is a story conveying the message of "AGAPE LOVE" as powerful as any scripture. Grace saves us by faith not of works lest any man should boast.

In this book, the parable of the father and his two sons is explored believing that the Holy Spirit will minister eternal truths to you as you read.

To make reading easy and focussed, should you not have a Bible at hand, I have included the KJV of the story just before the first chapter of this book. Other scriptures referred to in each chapter are quoted at the end of that chapter.

Grace or Works?

References

Genesis 25:5-6
⁵ And Abraham gave all that he had unto Isaac. ⁶ But unto the sons of the concubines, which Abraham had, Abraham gave gifts, and sent them away from Isaac his son, while he yet lived, eastward, unto the east country.

Genesis 27:27-29
²⁷ And he came near, and kissed him: and he smelled the smell of his raiment, and blessed him, and said, See, the smell of my son is as the smell of a field which the LORD hath blessed. ²⁸ Therefore God give thee of the dew of heaven, and the fatness of the earth, and plenty of corn and wine.
²⁹ Let people serve thee, and nations bow down to thee: be lord over thy brethren, and let thy mother's sons bow down to thee: cursed be every one that curseth thee, and blessed be he that blesseth thee.

2. *Leviticus 25:3-8*
³ Six years thou shalt sow thy field, and six years thou shalt prune thy vineyard, and gather in the fruit thereof; ⁴ But in the seventh year shall be a sabbath of rest unto the land, a sabbath for the LORD: thou shalt neither sow thy field, nor prune thy vineyard. ⁵ That which groweth of its own accord of thy harvest thou shalt not reap, neither gather the grapes of thy vine undressed: for it is a year of rest unto the land. ⁶

And the sabbath of the land shall be meat for you; for thee, and for thy servant, and for thy maid, and for thy hired servant, and for thy stranger that sojourneth with thee, ⁷ And for thy cattle, and for the beast that are in thy land, shall all the increase thereof be meat.
⁸ And thou shalt number seven sabbaths of years unto thee, seven times seven years; and the space of the seven sabbaths of years shall be unto thee forty and nine years.

3. Joshua 17:3-5
³ But Zelophehad, the son of Hepher, the son of Gilead, the son of Machir, the son of Manasseh, had no sons, but daughters: and these are the names of his daughters, Mahlah, and Noah, Hoglah, Milcah, and Tirzah. ⁴ And they came near before Eleazar the priest, and before Joshua the son of Nun, and before the princes, saying, The LORD commanded Moses to give us an inheritance among our brethren. Therefore according to the commandment of the LORD he gave them an inheritance among the brethren of their father.
⁵ And there fell ten portions to Manasseh, beside the land of Gilead and Bashan, which were on the other side Jordan;

Grace or Works?

The Parable

(Luke 15:11-32)

11. And he said, A certain man had two sons: ¹² And the younger of them said to his father, Father, give me the portion of goods that falleth to me. And he divided unto them his living.¹³ And not many days after the younger son gathered all together, and took his journey into a far country, and there wasted his substance with riotous living. ¹⁴ And when he had spent all, there arose a mighty famine in that land; and he began to be in want. ¹⁵ And he went and joined himself to a citizen of that country; and he sent him into his fields to feed swine.¹⁶ And he would fain have filled his belly with the husks that the swine did eat: and no man gave unto him. ¹⁷ And when he came to himself, he said, How many hired servants of my father's have bread enough and to spare, and I perish with hunger! ¹⁷ I will arise and go to my father, and will say unto him, Father, I have sinned against heaven, and before thee, ¹⁸ And am no more worthy to be called thy son: make me as one of thy hired servants. ¹⁹ And he arose, and came to his father. But when he was yet a great way off, his father saw him, and had compassion, and ran, and fell on his neck, and kissed him. ²⁰ And the son said unto him, Father, I have sinned against heaven, and in thy sight, and am no more worthy to be called thy son. ²¹

Grace or Works?

But the father said to his servants, Bring forth the best robe, and put it on him; and put a ring on his hand, and shoes on his feet: ^{22} And bring hither the fatted calf, and kill it; and let us eat, and be merry: ^{23} For this my son was dead, and is alive again; he was lost, and is found. And they began to be merry. ^{24} Now his elder son was in the field: and as he came and drew nigh to the house, he heard musick and dancing. ^{25} And he called one of the servants, and asked what these things meant. ^{26} And he said unto him, Thy brother is come; and thy father hath killed the fatted calf, because he hath received him safe and sound. ^{27} And he was angry, and would not go in: therefore came his father out, and -entreated him. ^{28} And he answering said to his father, Lo, these many years do I serve thee, neither transgressed I at any time thy commandment: and yet thou never gavest me a kid, that I might make merry with my friends: ^{29} But as soon as this thy son was come, which hath devoured thy living with harlots, thou hast killed for him the fatted calf. ^{30} And he said unto him, Son, thou art ever with me, and all that I have is thine. ^{31} It was meet that we should make merry, and be glad: for this thy brother was dead, and is alive again; and was lost, and is found.

Chapter 1

The Younger Son

The younger son knew the culture and tradition of his people yet he asked his father for his share of the estate not money. He must have then sold his share of the estate on leasehold, got the money and left. Selling the family property/inheritance didn't pose many problems to him, as the leasehold will expire by the year of Jubilee (Leviticus 25:23-28).[1] He was adventurous, fun seeking, and receiving his own inheritance was a passport for the life he craved. He had so many points in his favour such as money, possession and age (Proverbs 20:29a).[2]

Whilst he asked for his inheritance, there is no indication that the young man asked his father for permission to travel abroad. The Lord will give anyone, young or old, their own inheritance in Him if they ask. Unfortunately, when we ask and receive God's blessings, we many times fail to ask Him how to use such blessings, as God in His mercy has given us the free will to use those blessings as we like (Luke 19:13-21).[3]

THE TASTE OF SIN

Many today have left the good tradition of their people in search of, pleasure and adventure. Many have left the Father's kingdom for the world. Others who once knew, shared in, and enjoyed fellowship with the Lord have chosen to walk away from Him, His people, the Church, their families and gone to try the 'world'. They feel that God, the Bible, the Church and, or their families, especially their parents, are too strict with all the laws, rules, regulations and mandates or they are offended by their relationship with others in the Church.

What started as *"freedom at last"* from accountability to God, their families, especially parents, and the Church has now left them in chaos: lack of peace, bondage to sin, self and Satan, poverty within and around, physical, emotional, financial and spiritual sickness. All sins leave a bitter taste afterwards.

The young man left home with everything that was his to a distant country possibly trying to avoid being monitored by his father or anyone else (Proverbs 27:8).[4] How far away from God are you? The farther away you are from God, the farther you are from protection and the nearer to destruction.

In the distant country, the young man squandered his money in loose living. He possibly was naturally lazy as he did not initially consider nor try taking up a job. There is also no indication that he wrote home or contacted his father. He wanted to be anonymous and free in the distant country.

The young man did not understand the culture of the distant country he was in. He possibly thought that wining and dining could guarantee good friendship and lasting relationships. All the money he had was spent on parties and prostitutes and his wrong motives for travelling abroad came to light now that he was on his own (Proverbs 21:2).[5] He had definitely joined the wrong group, which eventually led to his downfall and poverty (Proverbs 31:2-7, 23:26-35; 1 Corinthians 15:33; Proverbs 18:24a).[6]

An affair these days with a prostitute is more dangerous and destructive than in Jesus' time. Just a fling or one-night stand can bring everlasting sorrow. A prostitute is a reservoir of greed; he or she could be a reservoir of diseases (all sexually transmitted disease, AIDS inclusive), of shame when found out, of poverty as every patronage with the prostitute costs money or possession and bitterness at the end. It takes God and self-discipline for one not to visit a prostitute (Proverbs 19:14a, 7: 6-27, 23: 27-28, 5:3-14; James 4:4).[7]

It's My Life

'It's my life' you say and you are correct
'I can live just the way I want and choose'
Sleeping all day instead of going to school or work
Watching the television twenty-four seven
Staying on the 'dole' instead of seeking for employment
Partying, clubbing instead of studying or working
Sleeping around with whomever and whenever
Instead of keeping your body a temple for God
Overeating instead of eating moderately
Overworking instead of taking adequate rest
It's my life you keep saying to yourself and others.

'It's my life' you say and you are correct
Friend, remember it is indeed your life
Once you choose your behaviour
You have chosen the reward of your behaviour
Time now to reconsider, time now to re-think
For you have just one life
Why end up in pain and shame?

Grace or Works?

Why live in abject poverty and starve,
When God has a better place and plan for you?
It's your life so make the best of it friend.

© *O. Ola-Ojo 14.06.08*

How true that many today think they can escape from God's watchful eyes. It is sad to see some young people from Christian homes whilst at higher institutions of learning or in foreign countries working or learning who desert their faith and Christian principles. They say, *"If you can't beat them, join them"* and so easily allow the negative culture of their new environment to influence them such that their own rich tradition and culture is abandoned. Time used previously for God is now used for non-God glorifying activities. They get lost in the crowd of sin and human wickedness; finally bringing shame, pain, hardship and disgrace to themselves and their families in many instances.

Children of God must be careful in their demands from God our heavenly Father and more careful of where they go, whom they chose as friends and what they do with their God-given possessions. Many will end up in hell because of their wrong motives and choice of friends (Proverbs 1:10, 14:12 and 16:25).[8]

As the wise saying goes, *"show me your friend and I will tell you your future."*

Drinking and partying will rob those who indulge in them of their respect, self-control and values. Drinking is a good source of health and wealth destruction. Alcohol leaves indulgers tipsy, liable to foul language, and untold injuries (Proverbs 20:1, 20-21, 21:17, 23:20-21, 23:29-35,).[9]

The Young Son

Everything that has a beginning surely has an end. A severe famine came when the young man's wealth had gone. It is so easy to spend one's life savings overnight or within a short time in riotous living. A severe famine does not suddenly occur, there must have been indications of this impending famine which the young man had ignored or had not been aware of (verse 14). In the same way, many are ignoring obvious financial and spiritual forecasts in their wasteful spending today. It is not too late to take stock to avoid famine.

The prodigal son did not prepare for the rainy day. It is sad that due to foolishness, he who was very wealthy became so poor to the point of starvation. His newly acquired foreign friends abandoned him and he was soon out of the group (Proverbs 20:21, 28:19, 16:25).[10]

Watch out, do you think you can outsmart the devil or people of the world? They are deep in sin, wickedness and have no pity or mercy. The devil attacks mostly when we are most vulnerable and he is out to strip any foolish person of all he or she have, turning the person over to loneliness, shame and want. Indeed the devil's apple is full of maggots. There is no real peace, joy or satisfaction in him. Asking for a legitimate right at the wrong time and for the wrong reasons, if care is not taken will lead to poverty and destruction.

The young man became hungry and had to attach himself to one of the citizens of that country who sent him into his field to feed the swine – i.e. pigs. Pigs are one of the animals forbidden by God for the Israelites to eat (Deuteronomy 14:7-8).[11] The young man was so hungry that feeding on the pig's pods seemed good to him but no one offered even that to him (Proverbs 27:7).[12]

Parties and prostitutes yea, a misspent life always ends up in loss of dignity. Life in a distant country could sometimes be frustrating especially where the culture of that strange land is not so caring to foreigners. Some out of poverty and hunger have done many 'unimaginable things' including selling themselves or their body parts, prostitution and selling members of their household. Should you be in such a position today, there is hope for you in Christ Jesus if you retrace your steps to Him. He is the way maker.

Leaving his father's territory exposed the young man to many dangers. There is untold misery and hardship for whoever strays away from the kingdom of God to the devils. Friend, never go anywhere or do anything that you cannot ask the Holy Spirit to bless (Proverbs 27:8).[13]

TIME TO RETURN

When the young man came to his senses, he remembered home, especially how wealthy and generous his father was such that even servants had more than enough to eat. The food he lacked in the distant country was abundant in his father's home! Whatever we are seeking for in life is in abundance in God and in our Father's home. It is only in God that there is the original satisfying joy, peace, love, protection, provision and wholeness.

One of the first steps to any recovery is to come to one's senses: take stock of the past and determine how things can get better.

For those who were once richly blessed of God but have lost it all due to their waywardness, there is no sin too terrible for God to forgive once you confess it. However deep in sin or distant

The Young Son

from home you might be, it is never too late to retrace your step. Your position in the Father's Kingdom remains. No matter how deep in sin and how far the sinner is or has backslidden from God, there is always the opportunity to take stock, recap life's experiences, analyze and re-evaluate the situation (James 4:8). [14] The fellowship might have been broken but the Father/child connection remains.

The young man decided that he had had enough outside of home, and made plans to return. How true is the saying that if one does not know where one is going, one certainly knows where one is coming from. He knew that if he confessed his sins, his father loved him, would forgive him and would be compassionate to him.

How much of God the Father do you know? Who is He to you? Do you know Him as:

Jehovah Jireh – your provider? – Genesis 22:8-14 [15]
El – Shaddai – your sufficiency? Genesis 22: 17 [16]
Jehovah Rohi – your shepherd? Psalm 23:1 [17]
Jehovah Shammar – ever present to you? Ezekiel 48:35 [18]
Jehovah Shalom – your peace? Judges 6:24 [19]
Jehovah Ropheka- your healer? Exodus 15:26 [20]
Jehovah Nissi – your banner? Exodus 17:15 [21]
Jehovah Adonai – your Sovereign God? Genesis 15:2-8 [22]

ACCEPT RESPONSIBILITY

The young man was humble enough to admit his sins and the severity of his mistakes against heaven and against his father. He realised that the authority of his father over him was from God. He considered his unworthiness to remain a son or to be addressed as such. To him, he had lost his sonship rights and was content to be just a servant for at least his meals would be guaranteed. That was his second chance and he was not going to miss it. He did not blame anyone for his misfortune. He took responsibility for his actions and for the outcome of his trip abroad.

The young man did not feel too big to return home to face his shameful past. The possible humiliation to follow as a servant where once he was a son could not deter his return. He had come to accept the fact that as a servant he would be required to work hard on the farm, with no more room for laziness or that much freedom as before. He must have realized that no place was like home where he understood the culture and the tradition and where he belonged. His experiences abroad were no match for the love and belonging at home.

He prepared a confession and an apology speech and acted immediately on his plans without procrastination. He retraced his steps back home. He who left loaded with his inheritance returned empty, raggedly dressed and devoid of all his wealth. All the same, that did not deter him from returning home. (Proverbs 28:13).[23] How many have procrastinated when they had another chance of beginning again and lost the opportunity. Procrastination they say is the enemy of time. Now is the time to be reconciled to your God and your family. Tomorrow may be too late. Seize the opportunity that is being offered to you now.

Friend one way home to God is the way of acceptance, repentance and confession of our sins and lost privileges. No one can impress God or get to heaven only by charity works, or being good. Jesus said He is the only way to God. Our repentances cause a big celebration in heaven. Friend, it is not too late to take stock of your life and return home to God through Jesus Christ. Return to the saving faith in Christ and return to the loving arms of your family in Church and at home.

The young man did not take his father's embrace for granted. His prepared and rehearsed speech was recited in repentance to his loving father. Not one word was omitted. Likewise, salvation and redemption are for those who see themselves the way God sees them, those who will not excuse any sin, however little, those who will believe in their inability to live successful lives on their own, those who will accept Christ's death on the cross for them (Romans 10:8-10; 1 John 1:9). [24] No one will be saved by childhood confirmation or baptism. A deliberate effort must be made to repent, to retrace one's steps back to God, confess whatever sins there are and accept Christ's redemptive work on the cross.

Now sensitive to his father's feelings, the young man did not in any way try to justify his actions, excuse his sins or pass the blame to anyone else. He approached his father just as he was, without one plea. Is your life like that reflected in this song? Please pause, read and meditate:

Just as I am

Just as I am, without one plea,
But that Thy blood was shed for me,
And that Thou bidst me come to Thee,
O Lamb of God, I come, I come.

Just as I am, and waiting not
To rid my soul of one dark blot,
To Thee whose blood can cleanse each spot,
O Lamb of God, I come, I come.

Grace or Works?

Just as I am, though tossed about
With many a conflict, many a doubt,
Fightings and fears within, without,
O Lamb of God, I come, I come.

Just as I am, poor, wretched, blind;
Sight, riches, healing of the mind,
Yea, all I need in Thee to find,
O Lamb of God, I come, I come.

Just as I am, Thou wilt receive,
Wilt welcome, pardon, cleanse, relieve;
Because Thy promise I believe,
O Lamb of God, I come, I come.

Just as I am, Thy love unknown
Hath broken every barrier down;
Now, to be Thine, yea, Thine alone,
O Lamb of God, I come, I come.

Just as I am, of that free love
The breadth, length, depth, and height to prove,
Here for a season, then above,
O Lamb of God, I come, I come!

Words: Charlotte Elliott, 1835; first appeared in The Christian Remembrance, whose editor Elliott became in 1836. The last verse is from Elliott's Hours of Sorrow Cheered and Comforted, 1836. Source://cyberhymnal.org

The Young Son

FORGIVENESS, RESTORATION AND CELEBRATION

Following his confession, the young man was forgiven and restored to his position as a son. In addition, his clothes were changed: the finest robe in the house was given to him. Such a robe was meant for the heir, and most beloved.

God is able to clothe the repenting sinner with His robe of redemption, love and protection. Compare with Joseph's robe in Genesis 37:3 [25], Queen Esther's robe in Esther 5:1-2 and Mordecai's robe in Esther 6:10 -11 [26].

Next was the ring placed on the young man's finger, a sign of the new relationship, covenant and authority (Genesis 41: 41-42; Esther 8: 2; John 1:12) [27] Then were the shoes for his weary feet, to protect him and keep him warm and possibly to spread the gospel about his father's love (Ephesians 6:15). [28]

Finally the fattened calf was killed and there was a party immediately to celebrate his homecoming. In like manner, Jesus Christ, the only Beloved Son of God had to be sacrificed in order for us to be accepted into the Kingdom of God. Just as it cost the father of the prodigal son his fattened calf, it cost God the precious life of His only Son for us to be redeemed from the power of sin into the commonwealth of His love and mercy.

Friend, when you come to Jesus Christ heaven celebrates this decision that you have made: there is rejoicing in heaven when someone becomes born-again (Luke 15:10). [29] It is because of John 3:16 [30] that we are forgiven and re-instated in God's kingdom. Without the shedding of blood there can be no remission of sin

Grace or Works?

(Hebrews 9:22). [31] The devil has nothing of eternal value to offer, but Christ has abundant life to offer to those who come to him.

For the sinner, societal acceptance is considered secondary to God's acceptance. Sinners want to impress peers not God. When David was confronted with the murder of Uriah the Hittite, he went before the Lord saying against Him had he sinned (Psalms 51). [32] Psalms 32:1-5.

However horrible the sin is, it is first against God that we have sinned since He is the Creator, Ruler and Father of all. All confessions must first be made to Him.

We need to forgive others and ourselves and be happy to receive the new status - cleansed and forgiven. Embrace the new relationship: that of sonship not servant hood and embark on a new trip with God. Complete surrender, obedience, demonstrating authority over Satan and his cohorts as part of the new life.

The young man readily accepted his father's forgiveness, the reinstatement and the party. Anyone who has confessed their sins in true repentance must be willing to accept the Lord's forgiveness without hesitation or reservation and so must the Church. Very importantly, you must forgive yourself for your painful sinful and past life.

Should you find your situation like that of the younger son and would want to experience a second chance from God; I invite you to solemnly say this prayer:

The Young Son

Dear Father,

I thank you for the opportunity that I have to read Your word and see my life in the light of Your written and Living Word. I confess that I have many times taken You for granted in many of my requests that I have made to you. I have also made selfish requests. I confess that I have deliberately walked away from my home and my Church Fellowship; I have been too busy and no longer have time to pray or spend quality time in Your presence, neither do I read or meditate upon Scriptures. With my granted request of my inheritance of wealth, good health, promotion or/ and family entanglements, I have acquired ungodly friends and associates. Lord, I confess my sins which are many and obvious to You including¬_____ (List them). Against You oh Lord, have I sinned. Lord, according to Your promises that whoever including myself who comes to You will never be cast away, I come to You Father in the name of Your Son, Jesus pleading for mercy, forgiveness and full restoration.

Father, thank You for accepting me just as I am and for forgiving me of all my iniquities and cleansing me from all unrighteousness.
I choose to forgive as many people who had wronged me in the process of my walk away from You Lord and also with Your Help choose to forgive myself.

Thank You Lord for yet another chance to experience Your love, security and blessings. Please keep me in the very hollow of Your Hands. Help me Father to obey You again and be of service to other people. Dear Lord, I humbly ask for the presence of Your Holy Spirit in my life from now on. Help me in every decision and action. Please teach me to know You, obey and follow You Lord from now. In Jesus name I pray. Thank You Lord for everything; in Jesus name I pray with thanksgiving. Amen.

Summary of Points about the young man:

- He was aware of his legitimate inheritance with his father.
- He asked his father for:
  - His share of wealth and inheritance
  - Forgiveness
- He was adventurous in:
  - Asking for his inheritance
  - Selling /leasing his inheritance
  - Travelling abroad
  - Living a loose life abroad
  - Feeding the pigs
  - Wanting to 'dine with the swine' if allowed.
- He had goals and worked to fulfil them:
  - Asking for his inheritance and subsequently travelling abroad
  - Retracing his steps back home and actually reciting his prepared and rehearsed confessional speech.
- He never procrastinated over his decisions and actions.

The Young Son

- He was initially insensitive but at the end was sensitive to his father's feelings.
- He remembered home when the going was tough.
- He knew his father and keyed into his attributes as:
  - Wealthy
  - A generous giver
  - Compassionate
  - Welcoming
  - Forgiving
  - Easily approachable
  - Very understanding
  - Caring
  - One who hears what is said and what is not said
- He openly admitted, confessed his sins and retraced his steps.
- He blamed no one for the turn out of his trip.
- He was humble to:
  - Go back home
  - Confess his sins without blaming anyone else
  - Accept the position of a slave
  - Now want to work
  - Accept his father's forgiveness
- He knew whom he had wronged most, heaven and his father. He didn't allow the possibility of his brother's rejection to deter him from asking his father for forgiveness.
- He gladly accepted his father's forgiveness and welcome party especially that of the shedding of the blood of the fattened calf.

Grace or Works?

MY PERSONAL NOTES

References

1. Leviticus 25:23-28

²³ The land shall not be sold for ever: for the land is mine; for ye are strangers and sojourners with me. ²⁴ And in all the land of your possession ye shall grant a redemption for the land. ²⁵ If thy brother be waxen poor, and hath sold away some of his possession, and if any of his kin come to redeem it, then shall he redeem that which his brother sold. ²⁶ And if the man have none to redeem it, and himself be able to redeem it; ²⁷ Then let him count the years of the sale thereof, and restore the overplus unto the man to whom he sold it; that he may return unto his possession. ²⁸ But if he be not able to restore it to him, then that which is sold shall remain in the hand of him that hath bought it until the year of jubile: and in the jubile it shall go out, and he shall return unto his possession.

2. Proverbs 20:29
The glory of young men is their strength:

3. Luke 19:13

¹³ And he called his ten servants, and delivered them ten pounds, and said unto them, Occupy till I come. ¹⁴ But his citizens hated him, and sent a message after him, saying, We will not have this man to reign over us. ¹⁵ And it came to pass, that when he was returned, having received the kingdom, then he commanded these servants to be called unto him, to whom he had given the money, that he might know how much every man had gained by trading. ^16 Then came the first, saying, Lord, thy pound hath gained ten pounds. ^17 And he said unto him, Well, thou good servant: because thou hast been faithful in a very little, have thou authority over ten cities. ^18 And the second came, saying, Lord, thy pound hath gained five pounds. ^19 And he said likewise to him, Be thou also over five cities. ^20 And another came, saying, Lord, behold, here is thy pound, which I have kept laid up in a napkin: ^21 For I feared thee, because thou art an austere man: thou takest up that thou layedst not down, and reapest that thou didst not sow.

4. Proverbs 27:8 *As a bird that wandereth from her nest, so is a man that wandereth from his place.*

5. Proverbs 21:2 *Every way of a man is right in his own eyes: but the LORD pondereth the hearts.*

6. Proverbs 31:2-7
^2 What, my son? and what, the son of my womb? and what, the son of my vows? ^3 Give not thy strength unto women, nor thy ways to that which destroyeth kings. ^4 It is not for kings, O Lemuel, it is not for kings to drink wine; nor for princes strong drink: ^5 Lest they drink, and forget the law, and pervert the judgment of any of the afflicted.

^6 Give strong drink unto him that is ready to perish, and wine unto those that be of heavy hearts. ^7 Let him drink, and forget his poverty, and remember his misery no more.

References

Proverbs 23:26-35
[26] My son, give me thine heart, and let thine eyes observe my ways. [27] For a whore is a deep ditch; and a strange woman is a narrow pit. [28] She also lieth in wait as for a prey, and increaseth the transgressors among men. [29] Who hath woe? who hath sorrow? who hath contentions? who hath babbling? who hath wounds without cause? who hath redness of eyes? [30] They that tarry long at the wine; they that go to seek mixed wine. [31] Look not thou upon the wine when it is red, when it giveth his colour in the cup, when it moveth itself aright. [32] At the last it biteth like a serpent, and stingeth like an adder. [33] Thine eyes shall behold strange women, and thine heart shall utter perverse things. [34] Yea, thou shalt be as he that lieth down in the midst of the sea, or as he that lieth upon the top of a mast. [35] They have stricken me, shalt thou say, and I was not sick; they have beaten me, and I felt it not: when shall I awake? I will seek it yet again.

1Corinthians 15:33 Be not deceived: evil communications corrupt good manners.

Proverbs 18:24a A man that hath friends must shew himself friendly:

7. *Proverbs 19:14* House and riches are the inheritance of fathers:

Grace or Works?

Proverbs 7:6-27

6. For at the window of my house I looked through my casement, 7 And beheld among the simple ones, I discerned among the youths, a young man void of understanding,

8 Passing through the street near her corner; and he went the way to her house, 9 In the twilight, in the evening, in the black and dark night: 10 And, behold, there met him a woman with the attire of an harlot, and subtil of heart. 11 (She is loud and stubborn; her feet abide not in her house: 12 Now is she without, now in the streets, and lieth in wait at every corner.) 13 So she caught him, and kissed him, and with an impudent face said unto him, 14 I have peace offerings with me; this day have I payed my vows. 15 Therefore came I forth to meet thee, diligently to seek thy face, and I have found thee. 16 I have decked my bed with coverings of tapestry, with carved works, with fine linen of Egypt. 17 I have perfumed my bed with myrrh, aloes, and cinnamon. 18 Come, let us take our fill of love until the morning: let us solace ourselves with loves. 19 For the goodman is not at home, he is gone a long journey: 20 He hath taken a bag of money with him, and will come home at the day appointed. 21 With her much fair speech she caused him to yield, with the flattering of her lips she forced him. 22 He goeth after her straightway, as an ox goeth to the slaughter, or as a fool to the correction of the stocks; 23 Till a dart strike through his liver; as a bird hasteth to the snare, and knoweth not that it is for his life. 24 Hearken unto me now therefore, O ye children, and attend to the words of my mouth. ²⁵ *Let not thine heart decline to her ways, go not astray in her paths.* ²⁶ *For she hath cast down many wounded: yea, many strong men have been slain by her.* ²⁷ *Her house is the way to hell, going down to the chambers of death.*

Proverbs 23:27-28 (see 6 above)

Proverbs 5:3-14
³ *For the lips of a strange woman drop as an honeycomb, and her mouth is smoother than oil:* ⁴ *But her end is bitter as wormwood, sharp as a two sedged sword.* ⁵ *Her feet go down to death; her steps take hold on hell.* ⁶ *Lest thou shouldest ponder the path of life, her ways are moveable, that thou canst not know them.* ⁷ *Hear me now therefore, O ye children, and depart not from the words of my mouth.* ⁸ *Remove thy way far from her, and come not nigh the door of her house:* ⁹ *Lest thou give thine honour unto others, and thy years unto the cruel:* ¹⁰ *Lest strangers be filled with thy wealth; and thy labours be in the house of a stranger;* ¹¹ *And thou mourn at the last, when thy flesh and thy body are consumed,* ¹² *And say, How have I hated instruction, and my heart despised reproof;* ¹³ *And have not obeyed the voice of my teachers, nor inclined mine ear to them that instructed me!* ¹⁴ *I was almost in all evil in the midst of the congregation and assembly. ask, and receive not, because ye ask amiss, that ye may consume it upon your lusts.*

Grace or Works?

James *4:4 Ye adulterers and adulteresses, know ye not that the friendship of the world is enmity with God? whosoever therefore will be a friend of the world is the enemy of God.*

8. Proverbs *1:10 My son, if sinners entice thee, consent thou not.*

Proverbs *14:12 There is a way which seemeth right unto a man, but the end thereof are the ways of death.*
Proverbs *16:25 There is a way that seemeth right unto a man, but the end thereof are the ways of death.*

9. Proverbs *20:1 Wine is a mocker, strong drink is raging: and whosoever is deceived thereby is not wise. Proverbs 20:20 Whoso curseth his father or his mother, his lamp shall be put out in obscure darkness. Proverbs 20:21 An inheritance may be gotten hastily at the beginning; but the end thereof shall not be blessed.*

Proverbs 21:17 He that loveth pleasure shall be a poor man: he that loveth wine and oil shall not be rich.
Proverbs 23:20 Be not among winebibbers; among riotous eaters of flesh: Proverbs 23:21 For the drunkard and the glutton shall come to poverty: and drowsiness shall clothe a man with rags.

References

Proverbs 23:29-35
[29] Who hath woe? who hath sorrow? who hath contentions? who hath babbling? who hath wounds without cause? who hath redness of eyes? [30] They that tarry long at the wine; they that go to seek mixed wine. [31] Look not thou upon the wine when it is red, when it giveth his colour in the cup, when it moveth itself aright. [32] At the last it biteth like a serpent, and stingeth like an adder. [33] Thine eyes shall behold strange women, and thine heart shall utter perverse things. [34] Yea, thou shalt be as he that lieth down in the midst of the sea, or as he that lieth upon the top of a mast. [35] They have stricken me, shalt thou say, and I was not sick; they have beaten me, and I felt it not: when shall I awake? I will seek it yet again.

10. (See note 9. above)

Proverbs 28:19 He that tilleth his land shall have plenty of bread: but he that followeth after vain persons shall have poverty enough.

Proverbs 16:25 There is a way that seemeth right unto a man, but the end thereof are the ways of death.

11. **Deuteronomy** 14:7

Nevertheless these ye shall not eat of them that chew the cud, or of them that divide the cloven hoof; as the camel, and the hare, and the coney: for they chew the cud, but divide not the hoof; therefore they are unclean unto you. Deuteronomy 14:8 And the swine, because it divideth the hoof, yet cheweth not the cud, it is unclean unto you: ye shall not eat of their flesh, nor touch their dead carcase.

12. Proverbs 27:7 The full soul loatheth an honeycomb; but to the hungry soul every bitter thing is sweet.

13. (See note 4 above)

14. **James 4:8** *Draw nigh to God, and he will draw nigh to you. Cleanse your hands, ye sinners; and purify your hearts, ye double minded.*

15. Genesis 22:8-14
⁸ And Abraham said, My son, God will provide himself a lamb for a burnt offering: so they went both of them together. ⁹ And they came to the place which God had told him of; and Abraham built an altar there, and laid the wood in order, and bound Isaac his son, and laid him on the altar upon the wood. ¹⁰ And Abraham stretched forth his hand, and took the knife to slay his son. ¹¹ And the angel of the LORD called unto him out of heaven, and said, Abraham, Abraham: and he said, Here am I. ¹² And he said, Lay not thine hand upon the lad, neither do thou any thing unto him: for now I know that thou fearest God, seeing thou hast not withheld thy son, thine only son from me. ¹³ And Abraham lifted up his eyes, and looked, and behold behind him a ram caught in a thicket by his horns: and Abraham went and took the ram, and offered him up for a burnt offering in the stead of his son. ¹⁴ And Abraham called the name of that place Jehovahjireh: as it is said to this day, In the mount of the LORD it shall be seen.

References

16. Genesis 22:17 That in blessing I will bless thee, and in multiplying I will multiply thy seed as the stars of the heaven, and as the sand which is upon the sea shore; and thy seed shall possess the gate of his enemies;

17. Psalms 23:1 The LORD is my shepherd; I shall not want.

18. Ezekiel 48:35 It was round about eighteen thousand measures: and the name of the city from that day shall be, The LORD is there.

19. Judges 6:24 Then Gideon built an altar there unto the LORD, and called it Jehovahshalom: unto this day it is yet in Ophrah of the Abiezrites.

20. Exodus 15:26 And said, If thou wilt diligently hearken to the voice of the LORD thy God, and wilt do that which is right in his sight, and wilt give ear to his commandments, and keep all his statutes, I will put none of these diseases upon thee, which I have brought upon the Egyptians: for I am the LORD that healeth thee.

21. Exodus 17:15 And Moses built an altar, and called the name of it Jehovahnissi:

22. Exodus 15:2-8
[2] The LORD is my strength and song, and he is become my salvation: he is my God, and I will prepare

him an habitation; my father's God, and I will exalt him. ³ The LORD is a man of war: the LORD is his name.

⁴ Pharaoh's chariots and his host hath he cast into the sea: his chosen captains also are drowned in the Red sea. ⁵ The depths have covered them: they sank into the bottom as a stone. ⁶ Thy right hand, O LORD, is become glorious in power: thy right hand, O LORD, hath dashed in pieces the enemy. ⁷ And in the greatness of thine excellency thou hast overthrown them that rose up against thee: thou sentest forth thy wrath, which consumed them as stubble.

⁸ And with the blast of thy nostrils the waters were gathered together, the floods stood upright as an heap, and the depths were congealed in the heart of the sea.

23. Proverbs 28:13
He that covereth his sins shall not prosper: but whoso confesseth and forsaketh them shall have mercy.

24. Romans 10:8-10
⁸ But what saith it? The word is nigh thee, even in thy mouth, and in thy heart: that is, the word of faith, which we preach; ⁹ That if thou shalt confess with thy mouth the Lord Jesus, and shalt believe in thine heart that God hath raised him from the dead, thou shalt be saved. ¹⁰ For with the heart man believeth unto righteousness; and with the mouth confession is made unto salvation.

References

1John 1:9 If we confess our sins, he is faithful and just to forgive us our sins, and   to cleanse us from all unrighteousness.

25. Genesis 37:3 Now Israel loved Joseph more than all his children, because he was the son of his old age: and he made him a coat of many colours.

26. Esther 6:10-11
[10] Then the king said to Haman, Make haste, and take the apparel and the horse, as thou hast said, and do even so to Mordecai the Jew, that sitteth at the king's gate: let nothing fail of all that thou hast spoken. [11] Then took Haman the apparel and the horse, and arrayed Mordecai, and brought him on horseback through the street of the city, and proclaimed before him, Thus shall it be done unto the man whom the king delighteth to honour.

27. Genesis 41:41 And Pharaoh said unto Joseph, See, I have set thee over all the land of Egypt. Gen 41:42 And Pharaoh took off his ring from his hand, and put it upon Joseph's hand, and arrayed him in vestures of fine linen, and put a gold chain about his neck;

Esther 8:2 And the king took off his ring, which he had taken from Haman, and gave it unto Mordecai. And Esther set Mordecai over the house of Haman.

John 1:12 But as many as received him, to them gave he power to become the sons of God, even to them that believe on his name:

28. Ephesians 6:15 And your feet shod with the preparation of the gospel of peace;

29. Luke 15:10 Likewise, I say unto you, there is joy in the presence of the angels of God over one sinner that repenteth.

30. John 3:16 For God so loved the world, that he gave his only begotten Son, that whosoever believeth in him should not perish, but have everlasting life.

31. Hebrews 9:22 And almost all things are by the law purged with blood; and without shedding of blood is no remission.

32. Psalms 51:1
¹ Have mercy upon me, O God, according to thy lovingkindness: according unto the multitude of thy tender mercies blot out my transgressions. ² Wash me throughly from mine iniquity, and cleanse me from my sin. ³ For I acknowledge my transgressions: and my sin is ever before me. ⁴ Against thee, thee only, have I sinned, and done this evil in thy sight: that thou mightest be justified when thou speakest, and be clear when thou judgest. ⁵ Behold, I was shapen in iniquity; and in sin did my mother conceive me. ⁶ Behold, thou desirest truth in the inward parts: and in the hidden part thou shalt make me to know wisdom. ⁷ Purge me with hyssop, and I shall be clean: wash me, and I shall be whiter than snow. ⁸ Make me to hear joy and

gladness; that the bones which thou hast broken may rejoice. ⁹ Hide thy face from my sins, and blot out all mine iniquities.¹⁰ Create in me a clean heart, O God; and renew a right spirit within me. ¹¹ Cast me not away from thy presence; and take not thy holy spirit from me. ¹² Restore unto me the joy of thy salvation; and uphold me with thy free spirit. ¹³ Then will I teach transgressors thy ways; and sinners shall be converted unto thee. ¹⁴ Deliver me from bloodguiltiness, O God, thou God of my salvation: and my tongue shall sing aloud of thy righteousness. ¹⁵ O Lord, open thou my lips; and my mouth shall shew forth thy praise. ¹⁶ For thou desirest not sacrifice; else would I give it: thou delightest not in burnt offering. ¹⁷ The sacrifices of God are a broken spirit: a broken and a contrite heart, O God, thou wilt not despise. ¹⁸ Do good in thy good pleasure unto Zion: build thou the walls of Jerusalem. ¹⁹ Then shalt thou be pleased with the sacrifices of righteousness, with burnt offering and whole burnt offering: then shall they offer bullocks upon thine altar.

Chapter 2

The Elder Son

Not much was said about the elder son in the story but we know he was hardworking, obedient to their father, respected the tradition and culture of his people. He appeared to be contended with staying at home. For whatever reasons, he did not ask his father for anything so he was not given anything out of the ordinary. Certainly this son was oblivious to his already settled inheritance with their father and he was unaware of their father's attributes and so did not key into them.

HAVE YOU ASKED GOD?

"And yet you have never given me a kid that I might merry with my friends." The elder son accused their father of not being generous towards him, whereas, he had never asked their father for anything. Perhaps because he thought their father would not grant his request. How often we fail to get blessed because we fail to ask from God? When we do not ask we do not receive (James 4:2b).[1] God desires us to be honest in our prayer requests and relationship with Him. He wants us to ask so that our joy in Him may be full (John 16:22 –24).[2] Open communication brings progress.

Grace or Works?

Many today would not ask God for their needs or wants because they think God is too busy for such 'small requests' but I dare say to such people that they are wrong, for God delights and longs for us to ask Him for things however small.

Some would not ask as they do not want to bother God. Others would not ask because they have never known God as the giver of every good gift. Every good gift is from God the Father of light. Because some have biological fathers who were not there for them or who never gave them anything beyond their basic needs, they think of God in the same way. They are grateful to God for the basics but they never ask for more.

Some believe that without their asking, God will automatically give them their needs and wants since He knows all things. How wrong they are. Only those that ask received.

Under normal circumstances parents are glad when their child asks for things within their financial capability. Asking, for parents, enhances bonding and parent/child relationship. It shows their child trusts them. It gives parents the opportunity to demonstrate a level of love and responsibility to that child.

Others don't ask God because they feel God's purpose is only for one or few things e.g. salvation not healing or prosperity etc. How wrong they too are. Our God is multifaceted and He will be to you what you know Him to be.

Others would not ask because they asked before and since God did not answer them then, they are afraid or ashamed to ask again in case they have their expectations crushed again. Such people need to ask always, in and out of season, until they hear God speak to them about their request.

The Elder Son

Even though he knew all that remained after his younger brother's departure was most likely his, this elder son did not ask their father for anything. The younger brother asked for selfish reasons and the father gave him. The elder son did not ask even though his desire was genuine enough – *"to merry with [his] friends."*

The word that the earth is the Lord's and the fullness thereof is no good if the child of God will not ask God for specifics (Matthew 7:7-8).[3] Friend, if the whole world were to ask God for all their requests, the bank of heaven would not go bankrupt; there will still be much more left in heaven's treasury. So go ahead and ask for your needs according to God's will.

There is a place for asking God for our needs and rewards. You have not because you ask not. When last did you fail to ask God for something specific according to His will but when you saw someone else having that which you had secretly longed for, you became jealous? God is not partial: for all who believe in Him are His children. He expects us to ask Him for our needs and rewards. In asking, God expects us to ask for specifics. For example, if you are asking for a car it is better that you include in your request what specific type of car and what gadgets/facilities you want in it. Suppose you are asking for a job, then let Him know what sort of job e.g. office or outside-office job, where and why, salary, what other aspects you would like to be included in the job package. When God invariably answers, then you will be sure that was what you asked for. In my experience and that of many others, God often exceeds our expectation when He grants our requests.

CHECK YOUR MOTIVE

It does appear that the elder son had the wrong motive in serving their father all those years. It is so sad to see some people active in the Church today who do not believe in God and eventually openly go on television to deny the existence of God. Some years back in England, a Church Priest went on television claiming he did not believe that God existed. For the many years that he had preached about the Almighty God he did not believe in Him or have a personal relationship with Him? We can justify our every action but God looks at our motives (Proverbs 16:2; 21:2).[4] Jesus once said that on the last day many will say how they served Him and worked miracles in His name but He will say to them, *"Depart from Me ye workers of iniquity"* (Matthew 7: 21-23).[5] The elder son failed to realise that to their father good relationship and fellowship with him was more important than service good as his service was. Brethren, this is the time for each one of us to re-examine our motive for serving God.

NOT BY WORKS BUT BY GRACE

"And I have never neglected a command of yours," the elder son said. He was being like the Pharisee counting on his good deeds and self-righteousness. Romans 3:23 says, *'All have sinned and come short of the glory of God.'* David said, *'Behold I was brought forth in iniquity and in sin did my mother conceive me'* (Psalm 51:5). The Bible says if God were to mark iniquity who could stand (Psalm 130:3)? And that the best of our righteousness is like filthy rags before God (Isaiah 64:6). By works shall no man be justified; we are saved by faith in Jesus Christ not of works lest any man should

The Elder Son

boast (Ephesians 2:9). Your charitable deeds/activities will not get you to heaven's gate let alone inside heaven but confessing all your sins and believing in Jesus' work of redemption will.

The elder son did not acknowledge that his anger or insensitivity to their father's feelings regarding his brother's return was sinful, for the Lord enjoins us to rejoice with those rejoicing. When that notorious sinner - be it armed robber, child abuser, wife/husband molester, prostitute, repented and came to Church what was your reaction? Brethren, we must be careful, there is no big sin or small sin before God. Sin is sin. It needs to be admitted and confessed. Breaking one commandment of God is as good as breaking all the commandments. It operates on the principle of all or none (Proverbs 20:9).[6]

"But when this son of yours came" (verse 30). How quick the elder brother was to disown his brother as he referred to him as *'this son of yours'*. How easily family members disown their relatives especially those regarded as the black sheep in the family. How quick the Church is sometimes in disowning a backsliding Christian.

"...who devoured your wealth with harlots." The elder son had not even seen his younger brother nor talked with him yet he had made up his mind about him; he was very judgmental (James 4:11a, 12; 5:9).[7] Whilst the elder son's assessment of his younger brother's life-style abroad may have been right, he certainly was the wrong person to complain about the consumed wealth (Jonah 4:11; John 5:21).[8] If it was true that his younger brother had been with harlots and yet could retrace his steps back home, that was enough reason to rejoice. The elder son did not appreciate the depth of the spiritual, yea, social or medical problems his brother

Grace or Works?

might have experienced and that his return home must have been by divine intervention.

We must learn to find out facts about a matter before taking sides or else we are may jump to the wrong conclusion. How do we react to corrupt or wicked people like harlots, thieves, murderers and prisoners, who genuinely admit, repent and confess their sins publicly? How do we react when suddenly these redeemed brethen whom we, not God, have condemned start to manifest the gifts of the Holy Spirit, which perhaps we don't have?

Are there not people in the Church today who evangelise and pray with hearts that fail to show love and concern towards those that have strayed in the past? We are quick to remember their previous life-style and we sometimes feel it is an act of injustice for God to forgive such people and make them entitled to the same privilege as us (Acts 9:10-16).[9]

Don't we, like the elder son stigmatise repented sinners and keep our distance from them even when we attend the same fellowship or Church? Where is Agape love when we act like the elder son? Judgement and punishment is for the Lord not for us because it is Him who has been offended most not us.

"You killed the fattened calf for him." The elder son did not take time to ask his father why he killed the fattened calf. He did not appreciate the principle of the blood sacrifice, which was fulfilled in Jesus Christ. He did not realize that without the shedding of blood, there can be no remission of sin (Hebrews 9:22b).[10] To the elder son, killing the fattened calf was too much just to celebrate a reunion with his wasteful brother.

The Elder Son

As Christians how do we react to a preacher whose message focus on the cross persistently? How do we react when the sermon goes on for ten to fifteen minutes longer than usual because the preacher is pleading with just one sinner to come forward and repent of his/her sins? How do we react to different forms of evangelism e.g. preaching in the street or in the public transport? How do we react to prison evangelism, child evangelism? How do we react to supporting home and foreign mission work?

Don't we like the elder son sometimes have a misplaced priority stemming from our insensitivity and lack of agape love when we give priority to redecorating the Church building or purchasing another new organ over giving the same amount or even less towards evangelism which will see more people saved (John 13:34-35)?[11]

The better we grasp the fact that the only thing that brings joy in heaven is when a sinner repents not when we give or serve, the more we will value the souls of sinners and rejoice when they become born again. That gives God the greatest joy and so must it give us too.

PARTIES CAN BE GODLY

The elder son's hidden love for merry making came out. He was just neither adventurous nor bold enough to ask that's why he had never had a party with his friends. He lived in the midst of plenty with opportunities for enjoyment yet he was in want.

To be a Christian does not imply being miserable. Praise, worship and love feasts are more for us than for people of the world. The world's parties are counterfeit of the real joyful party celebrations with friends and family in the Lord. God wants us to celebrate and have a good time in His presence and in Holy Ghost led parties. It is good to take time out with our friends and loved ones.

We must be careful not to get left out of the party because of jealousy and anger. No matter who repents, it will not diminish the Father's love for us or usurp our position in His kingdom nor our inheritance that is already settled in Christ Jesus as God's child. There is no justification or grounds for the lack of love of the elder brother for his younger brother neither will there be for anyone who behaves in a similar manner.

The father said to his elder son, *"my child, you have always been with me and all that is mine is yours."* This compassionate father seized the opportunity to remind the elder son of his inheritance in him. He acknowledged and appreciated the elder son's presence with him all the while. He, there and then, gave the elder son his inheritance – *"all that is mine is yours"* - even when the elder son had not asked.

As a person and as a Church, have we grasped the promise that all that is God's is ours in Jesus Christ? Jesus said *"all authority in heaven and on earth is mine"* and when He was leaving, He gave believers that same authority (Matthew 28:18-20; Mark 16:15-18; Luke 24: 47- 49; John 20:21-23).[12] It is disheartening to see children of God who don't know their full rights to God's divine power, authority, health, wealth and blessings. They walk as victims and not as victors, in shame instead of being conquerors, as paupers rather than possessors of all that is good and Godly.

The Elder Son

Have you caught a reflection of some aspects of yourself in this elder brother's attitude and you would like to experience a second chance from God? If yes, please say this prayer with me:

Dear Father,

Thank you for the opportunity I have had to read Your word and see my life in the light of Your written and living Word. I confess that I have many times thought and acted like this elder son. I have been hardworking in Your vineyard and faithful to the traditional/ denominational beliefs of my church. I have not asked You, Father for many things that I wanted. I confess that many times I did not make a demand on Your provision of all the good and great gifts that are available to me in Christ Jesus. I have failed to ask, seek or knock on the door of opportunity or blessing.

I confess my insensitivity to Your feelings as I often find it difficult to rejoice over sinners who repent, and my wrong attitude to the emotional and physical well being of such people. I confess my critical, judgemental and condemning attitude and unnecessary anger.

I confess my self-righteousness, pride and my lack of understanding of the principle of reconciliation by the shedding of the blood of Jesus Christ. I confess my jealousy of Your Grace to the sinner and the wrong feeling that You are pouring more blessing on such people than myself who has not left the Christian fold or Christian life.

I confess not knowing or being oblivious to much of Your Fatherly character. Father, I confess to You my concealed desires for the following blessings (name them) such that I could have had a praise party with my family and friends.

I confess and repent of all of my sins which are too many and obvious. Against You oh Lord have I sinned. Lord, according to Your promises that whoever —including myself - comes to God will never be cast away. I come to You Father in the name of Your Son, Jesus pleading for Your mercy, forgiveness and full restoration.

Father, in Your mercy, please forgive me and help me to accept sinners like You do, loving them and extending my hands of fellowship like You do Lord. Help me Lord from now to be honest in my communications and service to You Lord. I choose to forgive as many people whom You have forgiven and also with Your help I choose to forgive myself.

Thank You Lord for yet another chance to experience Your love, security and blessings. Please keep me in the very hollow of Your Hands. Help me Father to obey You again. Now that I know better and according to Your will, Father, I ask for the following blessings: (name them). For each of the blessings, family and friends will join me in praising You. Thank You Lord for everything in Jesus name I pray with thanksgiving. Amen.

Perhaps, like the elder son or self righteous one, you are still struggling if you should come into the party prepared for by God the Father, paid for by God the Son, Jesus Christ and guaranteed by God the Holy Spirit, becoming the very reason for the party? Please prayerfully meditate on the words of this two songs:

Softly And Tenderly

Softly and tenderly Jesus is calling,
Calling for you and for me;
See, on the portals He's waiting and watching,
Watching for you and for me.

Refrain

Come home, come home,
You who are weary, come home;
Earnestly, tenderly, Jesus is calling,
Calling, O sinner, come home!

Why should we tarry when Jesus is pleading,
Pleading for you and for me?
Why should we linger and heed not His mercies,
Mercies for you and for me?

Refrain

Grace or Works?

Time is now fleeting, the moments are passing,
Passing from you and from me;
Shadows are gathering, deathbeds are coming,
Coming for you and for me.

Refrain

O for the wonderful love He has promised,
Promised for you and for me!
Though we have sinned, He has mercy and pardon,
Pardon for you and for me.

Refrain

Come home, come home,
You who are weary, come home;
Earnestly, tenderly, Jesus is calling,
Calling, O sinner, come home

Words & Music: Will L. Thompson, in Sparkling Gems, Nos 1 and 2, by J. Calvin Bushey (Chicago, Illinois. Will L. Thompson & Company, 1880)

Source :http://www.cyberhymnal.org/htm/s/o/softlyat.htm

O Lord your Tenderness

O Lord Your Tenderness
Melting all my bitterness
O Lord I receive Your love. [2]

The Elder Son

O Lord, Your loveliness
Changing all my ugliness
O Lord I receive Your love.
O Lord I receive Your love.

Written by Graham Kendrick
Source:http://www.kidung.com/asing/o_Lord_Your_tenderness.htm

Summary of Points about the Elder Son:

- He respected the tradition – by not asking his own inheritance from their father whilst he was alive.
- He was hard working.
- He was contented with staying at home with his father.

BUT:

- He was unaware of his inheritance with their father.
- He worked hard alongside their father but did not know their father's attributes nor keyed into some of them.
- He did not ask so he did not receive.
- He was insensitive to his father's feelings and needs– did not rejoice with his father when the younger son returned home.
- He did not love or care about his brother's soul or physical and mental well-being.
- He was very judgemental and condemned his brother.
- He was unnecessarily angry.
- He was self-righteous, proud, and thought his right was by works and not by grace.
- He did not grasp nor understand the principle of reconciliation by the shedding of blood.

- He denied his brother by saying 'this son of yours'.
- He was filled with jealousy.
- He was not adventurous
- He concealed his desires from his father by not asking for a lamb to make merry with his friends. He failed to realise that just as there is a time for work so is there a time for celebration and party – the Godly way.
- He did not know many of their father's characteristics.
- He, like the younger brother, needed to seek his father's forgiveness, be reconciled to him, and be a part of the celebration party.
- He lived amidst plenty but was in every way poor.

Similarities between the Two Sons:

- Both were from the same father.
- The same father brought both up.
- Both misbehaved and were insensitive to their father's feelings at some point in their lives.
- Both needed their father's forgiveness: grace through the shedding of the blood of the fattened calf.
- Both had the freedom of expression before their father.
- Both had access to their father.
- Both experienced their father's unmerited love.

The Elder Son

Differences between the two Sons:

Elder Son	Younger Son
Culturally aware and abiding	Not culturally abiding
Conservative	Adventurous
Concealed his feelings	Expressed his feelings
Did not ask so did not receive	Asked and received
Workaholic	Initially lazy
Harboured resentment	No resentment
Lived locally	Travelled abroad
Did not confess his sins	Confessed his sins
Self righteous and holy	Sinner but repentant
Shut himself out of the party	Got into the party and became the reason for the party
Had all the father's remaining wealth yet lived on just enough	Lived rich with his share of wealth
Judgemental	Not judgemental
Depended on works	Depended on grace
Did not know many of his father's attributes	Knew many of his father's attributes
Initially sensitive to his father's feelings	At the end was more sensitive to his father's feelings

Grace or Works?

MY PERSONAL NOTES

References

1. **James 4:2b** ye fight and war, yet ye have not, because ye ask not.

2. *John 16:22-24*
^{22} And ye now therefore have sorrow: but I will see you again, and your heart shall rejoice, and your joy no man taketh from you. ^{23} And in that day ye shall ask me nothing. Verily, verily, I say unto you, Whatsoever ye shall ask the Father in my name, he will give it you. ^{24} Hitherto have ye asked nothing in my name: ask, and ye shall receive, that your joy may be full.

3. *Matthew 7:7-8*
^{7} Ask, and it shall be given you; seek, and ye shall find; knock, and it shall be opened unto you: ^{8} For every one that asketh receiveth; and he that seeketh findeth; and to him that knocketh it shall be opened.

4. **Proverbs 16:2** All the ways of a man are clean in his own eyes; but the LORD weigheth the spirits.

Proverbs 21:2 Every way of a man is right in his own eyes: but the LORD pondereth the hearts.

5. **Matthew 7:21-23**
^{21} Not every one that saith unto me, Lord, Lord, shall enter into the kingdom of heaven; but he that doeth the will of my Father which is in heaven. ^{22} Many will say

to me in that day, Lord, Lord, have we not prophesied in thy name? and in thy name have cast out devils? and in thy name done many wonderful works? ^{23} *And then will I profess unto them, I never knew you: depart from me, ye that work iniquity.*

6. **Proverbs 20:9** *Who can say, I have made my heart clean, I am pure from my sin?*

7. **James 4:11** *Speak not evil one of another, brethren... James 4:12 There is one lawgiver, who is able to save and to destroy: who art thou that judgest another?*

James 5:9 Grudge not one against another, brethren, lest ye be condemned: behold, the judge standeth before the door.

8. **Jonah 4:11** *And should not I spare Nineveh, that great city, wherein are more than sixscore thousand persons that cannot discern between their right hand and their left hand; and also much cattle?*

John 5:21 For as the Father raiseth up the dead, and quickeneth them; even so the Son quickeneth whom he will.

9. **Act 9:10-16**
^{10} *And there was a certain disciple at Damascus, named Ananias; and to him said the Lord in a vision, Ananias. And he said, Behold, I am here, Lord.* ^{11} *And the Lord said unto him, Arise, and go into the*

street which is called Straight, and enquire in the house of Judas for one called Saul, of Tarsus: for, behold, he prayeth, [12] *And hath seen in a vision a man named Ananias coming in, and putting his hand on him, that he might receive his sight.* [13] *Then Ananias answered, Lord, I have heard by many of this man, how much evil he hath done to thy saints at Jerusalem:* [14] *And here he hath authority from the chief priests to bind all that call on thy name.* [15] *But the Lord said unto him, Go thy way: for he is a chosen vessel unto me, to bear my name before the Gentiles, and kings, and the children of Israel:* [16] *For I will shew him how great things he must suffer for my name's sake.*

10. Hebrews 9:22 *And almost all things are by the law purged with blood; and without shedding of blood is no remission.*

11. John 13:34 *A new commandment I give unto you, That ye love one another; as I have loved you, that ye also love one another. John 13:35 By this shall all men know that ye are my disciples, if ye have love one to another.*

12. Matthew 28:18-20
[18] *And Jesus came and spake unto them, saying, All power is given unto me in heaven and in earth.* [19] *Go ye therefore, and teach all nations, baptizing them in the name of the Father, and of the Son, and of the Holy Ghost:* [20] *Teaching them to observe all things*

whatsoever I have commanded you: and, lo, I am with you always, even unto the end of the world. Amen.

Marks 16:15-18

[15] And he said unto them, Go ye into all the world, and preach the gospel to every creature. [16] He that believeth and is baptized shall be saved; but he that believeth not shall be damned. [17] And these signs shall follow them that believe; In my name shall they cast out devils; they shall speak with new tongues; [18] They shall take up serpents; and if they drink any deadly thing, it shall not hurt them; they shall lay hands on the sick, and they shall recover.

Luke 24:47-49

[47] And that repentance and remission of sins should be preached in his name among all nations, beginning at Jerusalem. [48] And ye are witnesses of these things. [49] And, behold, I send the promise of my Father upon you: but tarry ye in the city of Jerusalem, until ye be endued with power from on high.

John 20:21-23

[21] Then said Jesus to them again, Peace be unto you: as my Father hath sent me, even so send I you. [22] And when he had said this, he breathed on them, and saith unto them, Receive ye the Holy Ghost: [23] Whose so ever sins ye remit, they are remitted unto them; and whose so ever sins ye retain, they are retained.

Chapter 3

The Loving Father

This father was an immensely wealthy and generous man with many servants. His were the two sons, the obedient one and the fun seeking one. His older son suffered from bitterness and anger whilst the younger one suffered from the lust of the flesh (Galatians 5:16-21).[1] The younger one was initially selfish, lazy, and inconsiderate; the older one was lacking in mercy, full of bitterness, resentment, anger, and unloving. But this loving father understood both children and was able to accommodate their personalities. God the Father in His creativity has made no two people alike; even identical twins will exhibit some slight differences.

The father of the two sons gave freedom to both children without imposing his will on either of them (verses 12 & 31). In the same way, God loves us equally: in His presence we are of equal importance, irrespective of our race, background, sex or past. We all have the freedom of speech and the liberty to approach God anywhere and for anything. He is very accommodating of our weaknesses and failures.

Can you as a father say of a truth that there is freedom of speech and expression in your home or do you always impose your ideas on your spouse and children? Except you allow each of your children to freely express themselves, you are in danger of making them unnecessarily withdrawn and it will be difficult to know what is in their mind let alone correct them where they are wrong or encourage good thoughts slow and ambitions.

The loving father granted his younger son's request (verses 12 & 29). The request had cultural, spiritual, physical and emotional implications for both father and son. Granting the son's request would result in a loss of father-son relationship, which would cost the loving father much more than anything money could buy. For the young man, he had possibly counted the cost but was excited about an unsupervised adventure.

The father gave only to the son who asked of him. How are you doing with giving to your family especially your children? You may give without loving but you truly cannot love your family without giving to them. What do you give Dad - material resources or your time and talent? Who do you give to amongst your children, the one who keeps asking or the quiet one? You need to give to the child who asks but some children would just not ask, such children should be loved more and encouraged to ask from you the parent. Are you fond of not keeping your promises or not pulling your financial weight in the home as a father? That might make your sensitive children not ask for anything.

For anyone who has a responsibility over other peoples lives, may I ask how you are doing with your givings to them? Are giving out of love or otherwise?

The two sons came from this father's loins, similar upbringing but each grew up differently. How does one explain how a biological mother and father will have two or more children, bring them up under similar conditions yet one or more of the children will turn out right and the other(s) will not? Arguably, the genes will differ but having been nurtured under similar conditions and circumstances, one would expect that genes would not bring about that much difference. The predicament that the father of these two men found himself is even more common today.

In this day and age with extreme peer pressure and only few Godly mentors in families and the community at large, it may be difficult for a young person not to derail. Being surrounded and exposed to so many ungodly activities as we have today, derailment from good values is highly probable.

PRODIGAL PEOPLE

As there are prodigal children so are there prodigal fathers, mothers, husbands and wives.

Prodigal fathers
The prodigal father, may not be forth-coming in facing up to his responsibilities, walks away from his wife before or after the birth of a child or in a child's childhood. He was never there when the child was growing up, never taught the child anything, cared less for the child's feeding, upkeep or well being, perhaps never paid for his or her education or medications. Now the child by the grace of God, has graduated with a good job, he tries to find a place in the child's life that he previously rejected and despised.

Prodigal mothers
The prodigal mother gives birth to a child but for whatever reasons, not minding what will happen to the child, she abandons the child of her womb with the child's father to be looked after by anybody, perhaps maltreated by relatives, a step mother or step siblings. The child never knew or experienced the love of a caring

mother. The child might have lived with the guilt that he or she must have caused the Mum so much pain and havoc and that is why she left him or her. The child's self worth is damaged and the child carries so much emotional baggage of fear, lack of true love and inability to trust anyone.

Prodigal husbands

The prodigal husband like the prodigal father leaves at the time he is most needed under some flimsy excuse. He leaves the woman with unpaid bills and mortgage, and forces her to join the statistics of single mothers who are barely able to make ends meet, playing the dual role of mother and father to their children) in spite of her other engagements and committments. He might have left her for a younger perhaps more beautiful or wealthy woman. He might have left without looking back, making no contacts to inquire about the physical, financial, emotional, social or spiritual well being of his children or their mother. Now that she has, by the grace of God sorted out herself and the children, the prodigal husband decides to return, perhaps in abject poverty, to this lady the first love of his life.

Prodigal wives

The prodigal wife walks out on the man with her husband's own friend or a wealthier man or any other man. His pleas and cries are not enough to make her change her mind. She knows she is all that her husband has, yet she leaves him when he is most vulnerable. On the other hand, she may still live in his home, but prostitutes herself to the richer man who may be known or unknown to her husband. Now like the prodigal son, she returns when no other man wants her and she has probably caught a deadly disease.

The Loving Father

As a parent, relative or spouse of the person who has wandered away like the prodigal son what is your immediate and general reaction to this person? Is it that of condemnation: 'After all that I/we did for you?' or that of 'See the shame and reproach that you have brought to the family?' or that of 'You have disgraced me/us' an outright rejection 'You are no good and therefore rejected' or do you belong to the redeemed and reconciliatory, or ask 'Where did I/we go wrong'?

Should your loved one selfishly walk away from you, I suggest that you prayerfully meditate on the words of this song:

Father I Place Into Your Hands

Father, I place into Your hands
The things I cannot do
Father, I place into Your hands
The things that I've been through
Father, I place into Your hands
The way that I should go
For I know I always can trust You.

Father, I place into Your hands
My friends and family
Father, I place into Your hands
The things that trouble me,
Father, I place into Your hands
The person I would be
For I know I always can trust You.

Grace or Works?

Father, we love to see Your face
We love to hear Your voice
Father, we love to sing Your praise
And in Your name rejoice
Father, we love to walk with You
And in Your presence rest
For we know we always can trust You.

Father, I want to be with You
And do the things you do
Father, I want to speak the words
That you are speaking too
Father I want to love the ones
That You will draw to You
For I know that I am one with you.
Jenny Hewer Copyright 1975 Kingsway Thank you Music

DON'T GIVE UP

The Bible says *'train up your child in the way he should go and when he is old, he will not depart from it'* (Proverbs 22:6).[2] But what do you do when the child you have trained in the way of the Lord years decides to abandon your faith, your God and Godly principles to launch into a foreign land of sin, self, and satanic practices? What do you do when your child leaves home for a far country and deliberately cuts off all family contacts?

How do you face your friends and family? What do you say to them? Should you lie to them and pretend that all is well or should you pour out your heart to them? What do you do as a parent when one or more of your children whom you have invested your

The Loving Father

life and wealth in, turns out to be like the younger son of the loving father?

Having to deal with a prodigal child, husband, wife, father or mother can be very daunting. Be encouraged, for as long as that person is alive there is hope. There are lessons to learn from the story of the loving father.

This father was very wealthy and could have sent his servants or spies after his prodigal son but he chose not. Not for lack of love but there comes a time when every one should be allowed to make their choices. God in His mercy has created us and given us the opportunity to be who we choose to be.

Although he didn't send a search party after his wayward son, this father never gave up on him; he daily and patiently waited for his son's return. Parents, which of your children have you given up on and why? It is possible for the once seemingly black sheep of the family to have his/her life turned around and become caring and responsible. One day the loving father's waiting paid off.

"But when he was yet a great way off, his father saw him, and had compassion, and ran, and fell on his neck, and kissed him." .He recognised his son from a great way off. In the same way Jesus knows His own, His sheep and His own knows Him. The son was still a great way off, yet his father saw him! Why? Because he was very watchful and in his heart, he knew his run away son would return. How could he be so sure? Because:

- He knew he had trained his son enough such that departing from his training and remaining in a strange land forever will be impossible.
- He knew he had shown his son so much love at home that

couldn't be paralleled elsewhere. How much love have you shown your child that would make them come back home especially when they run into trouble? A song says, *"The love He's shown couldn't make me think He'll leave me in trouble."*

- He knew his son was on a journey to a *'dead end'* and would soon realise it and retrace his steps back home.
- He knew the outcome of such demands by his experience of life – a life from home for his son could not be forever. An African adage says when young people are felling trees in the forest; the onlooking elders already know where the cut tree will fall. Age and life experience made this father able to predict the young man's return.
- He knew his son was sure of a place at home whenever he returned and that the young man would come back.
- He knew he had an open and healthy communication with his son, though the son acted wrongly causing him some pain and shame, yet he did not curse or disallow him from going away to try the world nor did he tell him not to return once he left his home.
- He was a prayerful father who walked by faith and not by sight. He acted on his faith. Father, though your son is far away from home in rebellion, lust, greed or other sin, please don't give up on him for your active faith will soon be rewarded.
- He knew his son enough to be able to predict him. Dad, how well do you know your child to be able to predict him/her?

This father had compassion, and ran, and fell on his younger son's neck, and kissed him. He had compassion not a mind of anger or revenge and he was not spiteful, judgmental or condemning. His assessment of his son from afar conveyed the hardship the

The Loving Father

young man had probably gone through. He couldn't wait for the son to get to him but ran to meet him. Whilst in religion, mankind is seeking to get to God, in Christianity which is a way of life, our heavenly Father reaches out to draw us into His love and presence. The father embraced his son. As dirty, tattered, unworthy of his love and smelly as his son was, he kissed him – a warm welcome back home and kind gesture to the undeserving young man. In love he gave him the opportunity to confess and apologize. This father was full of mercy and grace towards his prodigal child. He forgave and restored his runaway child to the full position of a son. To the father the younger son will always be a son never to be a slave or servant.

The father said to his servants, *"Bring forth the best robe, and put it on him; and put a ring on his hand and shoes on his feet:"* He asked that the young man be clothed in the best robe available. God's love, like snow, completely covers our sins and ugliness. The father covered his son's shame and, ugliness from the on looking world with the best robe available.

Fathers do you expose your already weak, feeble, dejected, vulnerable child to the world or do you cover his or her shame in prayers, love, acceptance and provision?

Note that the father did not subject the prodigal son to a period of testing but believed in him and protected him from the on looking, possibly sneering neighbours.

He threw a party, kill the fattened calf to welcome his lost son home.

Heaven rejoices when a sinner through the blood sacrifice of Jesus Christ returns to God by accepting salvation through grace not through works.

Grace or Works?

When your runaway child comes to his or her senses and you have lovingly forgiven and taken him or her back, it's time not only to rejoice and celebrate with a party but to cover that child's nakedness and restore him or her to the full position of sonship for all to see.

When the elder brother reacted to his father's lavish welcome of his wasteful younger brother, the loving father handled the situation wisely. He understood both his children and was able to accommodate their personalities. He went out of his way to meet each of them at their points of weakness (Verses 22, 28b, 31).

Parents, how much do you know about your children, their disposition and character and their goals for life?

How well do you understand each of your children and how are you able to accommodate their personalities? In what ways have you gone out to meet each of your children at their points of need and weakness? Take time today and begin to get to know each of your children at their points of weakness. Please come out practically in acts of love and mercy and if you can't reach the child directly because you are in different locations, then reach him on your knees in prayers. Remember that no child, however bad, is beyond God's love and redemption.

Salvation and redemption are very costly to God the Father, none the less both are available through Jesus Christ His only Son who died on the cross to pay the price for our sins (John 3:16).[3] Much as God loves the sinner, salvation is by faith and open confession of faith in Christ. (Romans 10:9, 10; John 3:17–18).[4] God the Father will save all who ask Him to, hence He gives each person the freewill to do what they like with such gifts (Luke 19:12-24).[5]

The Loving Father

God the Father is still looking out for any sinner who will repent of their sins. He never gives up on any sinner and is always going out to meet each person at their point of weakness. In the same way, the living Church of God must be concerned with lost souls and actively look out for them, reach out to them, never give up on any one.

It is not uncommon for parents to feel guilty when their child has willingly and knowingly walked away from the training and teaching they gave the child. They may feel guilty for *'not doing enough'* or *doing 'too much'* in times past. Parents may feel inadequate to provide any protection especially where the child in question is endangering his/her life and perhaps that of other friends and colleagues. Many have acquired diseases like high blood pressure, heart problems and depression because of their prodigal child or relative or husband or wife or sibling or parent. No prodigal person, however close, is worth getting ill over or dying for. As long as that person is alive there is hope.

MAKING THINGS RIGHT

Rather than becoming ill, physically, financially, emotionally or psychologically the following are some useful suggestions though not in any particular order:

- Go before God in humility and pour out your heart to Him confessing any sins or wrong doing on your part. Once God has forgiven you, you have no reason not to forgive yourself.
- Ask God through the Holy Spirit for wisdom on how to love your child in spite of the changed behaviour/lifestyle.
- In your mind and attitude, difficult as it may be, forgive that child. If God does not deal with us when we fall short on the

basis that we have brought Him shame despite all that He has done for us, then none of us has the right to use such a yard stick on others. 'He has not punished us as our sins deserve; He has not repaid us for the evil we have done. As high as the sky is above the earth, so great is His love for those who respect Him. He has taken our sins away from us as far as the east is from west (Psalm 103: 10–12).[6]

- Reason with your child pointing out the possible consequences of his or her decisions now and in the future.
- Difficult as it may be, love that child unconditionally.
- If it is possible, spend time alone with that child listening to him or her. Ask the child for forgiveness where you or your spouse have been part of the reason for the changed behaviour. This is not the time to argue or defend your wrong behaviour rather, be humble enough to accept the responsibility for the wrong and ask the child for forgiveness and correct yourself appropriately.
- If the child is not willing to talk to or with you, go on your knees in humility and talk to God the creator of that child.
- Seek for Godly counsel without delay. A stitch in time saves nine and saves time.
- Identify about three Godly people who can pray confidentially with you and the family in this storm and contact them immediately.
- Try to befriend your child's friends, invite them into your home. Observe them without any suspicion. You can understand your child through these friends and associates as you lovingly relate to and with them.
- Intercede for the soul of your child and friends. Praying without ceasing.
- Keep your doors open for your child to come back if and when he or she is ready to do so.

The Loving Father

- Though the age of maturity in many cultures/countries is 18, you don't have to send your errant child away if he or she is not a danger to your life or the life of others.
- When you have done all that needs to be done and your child still decides against your Godly advice – let go of that child in a pleasant way and let that child know that your door of warm love is always open. You cannot and must not try to live your life and dreams through your children or any other person.
- Don't give up on that wayward, backslidden child. God is able to turn him/her around. Don't give in to Satan. Win your child back on your knees with fervent intercessory prayers.

Many prodigal persons return home. Are you emotionally as well as in other ways prepared to forgive and welcome them back home? If you are not, perhaps it is time to prayerfully work on your self in anticipation of this glorious re-union. Are we as a Church ready for the big harvest of souls thirsting for God? What are we doing in this respect to make God happy and make heaven rejoice? We must remember the Lamb has been sacrificed, it is party time, the time to celebrate the return of all prodigals into His kingdom.

You can only give what you have. Do you have Jesus Christ in your life? Do you know the love and forgiveness of God? Do you have in you the Holy Spirit, author of love and teacher with the best wisdom? If not then you need to get yourself sorted out first and as you moment by moment rely on God He will help you.

Just before we end our look at the life of the father with the two sons, should you be a parent and one or more of your children have deliberately or otherwise walked away from home or from the godly faith in which you brought them up, I suggest that you say this prayer:

Grace or Works?

Dear Father,

Thank You for the opportunity that I have to read Your word and see my life in the light of Your written and living word. Thank you for the privilege of parenting my child. Thank You Lord for the child is Yours in the first instance. Lord, You know the pains and the agony of not knowing where my child is. I often feel that it's my fault for the way things are at present and do sincerely confess any of my known and unknown parental faults such as (mention them).

Lord, I am scared of my child's safety with unknown friends in an unknown and unsupervised environment. Lord, please help me not to give up on my child's safety and safe return home to us and to the gathering of believers. Lord please create in me in advance, a loving and forgiving spirit full of mercy and grace, that equally allows me to be restored fully with my child. Help me Lord to lovingly support my child's return to Jesus Christ. Teach me oh Lord, all that I need to be a living example of the parent You created me to be.

I choose to forgive as many people who have wronged me in the process of this experience and also with Your Help, I choose to forgive myself.

Thank You Lord for yet another chance to experience Your love and once again be an example

The Loving Father

of a Godly parent. Please keep my child and me in the very hollow of Your Hands. Thank You Lord for everything in Jesus name I pray with thanksgiving. Amen.

Now that God has helped you deal with that, please pick up the phone, or pen to write, make an effort to contact that prodigal child, not fault finding or apportioning blame but seeking for healing and enhancing good parental relationship.

I would like to say this prayer for you:

May the Lord send you:
Clarity in your disarray
Comfort in your pains
Courage in your despair
Faith in your fear
Healing in your sickness
Healing in your heartache
Hope in your hopelessness
Joy in your sorrow
Justice in your injustice
Light in your darkness
Peace in your troubles
Wisdom in your confusion
Love where and when you are hated
In the name of Jesus Christ. Amen.

Grace or Works?

MY PERSONAL NOTES

References

1. Galatians 5:16-21

[16] This I say then, Walk in the Spirit, and ye shall not fulfil the lust of the flesh. [17] For the flesh lusteth against the Spirit, and the Spirit against the flesh: and these are contrary the one to the other: so that ye cannot do the things that ye would. [18] But if ye be led of the Spirit, ye are not under the law. [19] Now the works of the flesh are manifest, which are these; Adultery, fornication, uncleanness, lasciviousness, [20] Idolatry, witchcraft, hatred, variance, emulations, wrath, strife, seditions, heresies,[21] Envyings, murders, drunkenness, revellings, and such like: of the which I tell you before, as I have also told you in time past, that they which do such things shall not inherit the kingdom of God.

2. Proverbs 22:6 Train up a child in the way he should go: and when he is old, he will not depart from it.

3. John 3:16 For God so loved the world, that he gave his only begotten Son, that whosoever believeth in him should not perish, but have everlasting life.

4. Romans 10:9

[9] That if thou shalt confess with thy mouth the Lord Jesus, and shalt believe in thine heart that God hath raised him from the dead, thou shalt be saved. [10] For

with the heart man believeth unto righteousness; and with the mouth confession is made unto salvation.

John 3:17-18
¹⁷ For God sent not his Son into the world to condemn the world; but that the world through him might be saved. ¹⁸ He that believeth on him is not condemned: but he that believeth not is condemned already, because he hath not believed in the name of the only begotten Son of God.

5. Luke 19:12-24
¹² He said therefore, A certain nobleman went into a far country to receive for himself a kingdom, and to return. ¹³ And he called his ten servants, and delivered them ten pounds, and said unto them, Occupy till I come. ¹⁴ But his citizens hated him, and sent a message after him, saying, We will not have this man to reign over us. ¹⁵ And it came to pass, that when he was returned, having received the kingdom, then he commanded these servants to be called unto him, to whom he had given the money, that he might know how much every man had gained by trading. ¹⁶ Then came the first, saying, Lord, thy pound hath gained ten pounds. ¹⁷ And he said unto him, Well, thou good servant: because thou hast been faithful in a very little, have thou authority over ten cities. ¹⁸ And the second came, saying, Lord, thy pound hath gained five pounds. ¹⁹ And he said likewise to him, Be thou also over five cities. ²⁰ And another came, saying, Lord, behold, here is thy pound, which I have kept laid up

in a napkin: ²¹ *For I feared thee, because thou art an austere man: thou takest up that thou layedst not down, and reapest that thou didst not sow.* ²² *And he saith unto him, Out of thine own mouth will I judge thee, thou wicked servant. Thou knewest that I was an austere man, taking up that I laid not down, and reaping that I did not sow:* ²³ *Wherefore then gavest not thou my money into the bank, that at my coming I might have required mine own with usury?* ²⁴ *And he said unto them that stood by, Take from him the pound, and give it to him that hath ten pounds.*

6. Psalms 103:10-12
¹⁰ *He hath not dealt with us after our sins; nor rewarded us according to our iniquities.* ¹¹ *For as the heaven is high above the earth, so great is his mercy toward them that fear him.* ¹² *As far as the east is from the west, so far hath he removed our transgressions from us.*

Chapter 4
Grace or Works?

Many believe in working for all that they have or own. That is a good philosophy to a certain extent in that if care is not taken, a self-sufficient attitude will develop and the person thinks, *"Why will I need God?"* Such a person finds it difficult to accept any free gift and thinks why do I need a free gift when I can work for it and be happy; I am not poor or disabled so why do I need anyone's free gift? Working for what we have is good so long as we don't get to the stage where we think we can be self sufficient – without God.

When it comes to salvation, the Bible is very clear about it for it says without the shedding of blood there can be no remission of our sins (Hebrews 9:22). Jesus also said no one comes to the Father except by Him (John 6:44). In John 3:16-18, we are told, *"for God so loved the world that He gave His only begotten son that whoever believes in Him should not perish but have everlasting life"*. The key to salvation is to accept that we are sinners not good enough for heaven, the best of our works is like filthy rags before the Almighty God and there are not enough riches in this world to redeem a soul from hell, so we all need Jesus to be our Lord and Saviour.

One just only one-way leads home to God. It is the way of accepting our sins, repenting of them and confessing them to our Father. Coming to Him just as we are, not on account of our looks or works for by works shall no man be justified.

Grace or Works?

Are there not people who are always willing and eager to give but unwilling to receive? Years ago, after a series of painful experiences, the Holy Spirit told me that anyone who is not willing to receive is not fit to give. Why be involved in charity or charitable activities and reject God's own Son's redemptive offer of love to you?

The person that operates by grace has come to the realisation that he or she cannot be good enough to qualify for the least of God's blessing including salvation.

That person is willing to receive all that God has provided through Jesus Christ with a heart of gratitude. Grace makes one glide into God's unlimited favour. Someone translated grace to be an acronym for God's Riches or Resources At Christ's Expense. A wise person has once said a gift is only a gift when it has been accepted. We receive God's grace by faith. Indeed, it is not of works lest any many should boast (2 Corinthians 10:8).

The blood of the lamb has been shed for our sins and the party has begun. There is room for all but you need to make the choice. Dear reader and friend, what is your choice - grace or works? I pray that you will choose right!

Grace or Works?

MY PERSONAL NOTES

CHAPTER 5

More Poems To Inspire You

The Dead End

*It starts like any other road
It looks beautiful and attractive
promising at the beginning
with signs to a destination.*

*What an unfortunate mistake to travel on it.
What seemed attractive and beautiful
unending and everlasting
Turns out to be one dead end.*

*Every sin dear friend is a dead end
For in the end it is full of disgrace and regrets
Full of heartaches, uncertainty and hatred.
Full of bitterness, pity and unaccountable loss.*

*No matter how small or big,
No matter where, when and how it was committed
No matter the excuse we want to give,
It does not remove sin from being a dead end.*

Grace or Works?

Now is the time to retrace your steps
Now is the time to reassess the situation
Now is the time to seek the Lord's face once more
In order not to end up in the dead end.

The dead end has nothing to offer
It has no guarantee, no security nor peace
It has no degree of commitment or improvement
It has no hope for a better future.

In your daily walk in life
Do try and watch out for dead ends
Do not be attracted to it or trapped in it
For in the end it is going to be what it is, the dead end.

© O.Ola –Ojo 11.03.92

Poems

Conquering the Problem

Many methods of getting rid of problems,
But first, recognise what the problem is
Prayerfully search the scriptures to know how best to overcome.

Moses at the Red Sea, stretched forth the anointed rod
Created dry land in the sea for the children of Israel to pass through
The same rod returned the sea, destroying Pharaoh and his hosts.

The Jericho wall, an obstacle to entering the Promised Land
was marched round once in six days, seven times on the seventh
With a loud shout unto the Lord, it all came crumbling down.

Arrogant, experienced, boastful Goliath at war with the Israelites
Confronted by little, inexperienced but Godly David in the Name of the Lord
With five stones and a sling, Goliath fell and was beheaded with his own sword.

The prophet's widow and her two sons at the creditors' mercy
Sought Elisha for God's counsel in her trouble
Obedience to divine counsel provided the needed money and much more.

Grace or Works?

The prodigal son coming back to his senses, realised his mistake
Retraced his steps home to his father in repentance and humility
He was completely forgiven, restored and reinstated.

The stormy sea, threatening to capsize the disciples' boat
Made them wake up Master Jesus who was asleep in the boat
He rebuked the wind, calmed the storm and peace was restored to the trip.

Jehoshaphat and his people attacked by a large army in evil confederacy
Took their places, stood quietly watching God's miraculous deliverance
As they sang loud and clear songs of praises to the Lord who is mighty in battle.

As you face the problem beloved, recognising what it is all about
You might have to confess, repent and retrace your steps back to God
You might have to apply the word of God, which is the sword of the Spirit
You might have to march round it in quietness and obedience to God's command.

You might have to attack it boldly like David in the name of the Lord
You might have to seek for counsel from God's anointed ministers

Poems

You might have to rebuke all the forces of attack in Jesus'
Name.

You might have to joyfully praise the Lord and watch the
enemies' defeat
Beloved, with God on your side,
You can face and conquer that problem.

©O.Ola-Ojo 14/11/91
2Chronicles 20: 1-23, 1Samuel 17: 1-54, Joshua 6: 1-25, Exodus.14: 1-31, 2Kings 4: 1-7, Mark 4:35-41, Luke 15: 11-24

Grace or Works?

Facing the Past

*What can be more disturbing
Than to face difficult situations
which you thought you had totally overcome
Jacob the sup planter, for fear of Esau ran to Uncle Laban*

*There he raised a family of four wives, many children
and great livestock
But the time came at last to return home to Canaan
Now after twenty years, to face his brother Esau whom he had
cheated twice.*

*Moses, in fear of being killed for murdering the Egyptian
Ran away to the land of Midian
For forty years he lived there and even raised a family
Alas,
God called him to return to Egypt and face Pharaoh.*

*Jonah, in disobedience boarded a ship to Tarshish
Thought he had evaded God's missionary call to Nineveh
but landed in the belly of a fish for three days in the sea
later to end up on the very shores of Nineveh.*

*Joseph's brothers in jealousy sold him to the Midianites
For over a decade they assumed they had gotten rid of him
Years of famine later brought them to Joseph
The reality of which left them in fear of him.*

Poems

For Joseph, the reunion with his brothers was traumatic
In love, he forgave their wickedness
He looked at the good their evil had brought,
And made adequate provision for the family's resettlement.

Paul, once a persecutor of the Church of God
His mission to Damascus changed his life and mission
No longer an accuser of the brethren but a brother and friend
Lived to face the many threats of the Jews.

Face it!
Face that part of your life that you thought was finally dead and gone.
Forgive what you need to forgive
Forgive who you need to forgive
Boldly face the situation
And watch God give you the victory.

Be reassured, God is able to turn
Your fears to faith
Your failures to fulfilment
Your mistakes to miracles.

Now is the moment to give Him all the praise!

© O. Ola - Ojo. 7/9/92.

Sin

How do you define sin, dear friend?
Have you removed the word from your dictionary?
Has it become one of those acceptable societal norms?

Sin to me, is not an illness, dear friend,
It is not a temptation nor problem,
It is not a mistake or normal,
It is that which is done of our choice.

Sin has a love, hate relationship,
Men tend to love its false pleasures,
Hating themselves, or others, thereafter,
It is that which requires forgiveness.

Sin is dabbled into deliberately and consciously-
It becomes addictive over time like a drug.
It never satisfies, no matter how much.
It tends to be covered up with other sins.

Sin is incredibly destructive, dear friend
It is the most expensive thing in this world,
It causes sickness and death of all kinds,
It finally sends the unrepentant sinner to Hell's fire.

Sin causes a person untold loss of relationship
It causes breaks in human relationships;
It breaks down communication with God;
It causes one to lose one's peace, respect and dignity.

Poems

Sin, expensive, as it was, had to be purchased,
It cost God His only begotten Son Jesus Christ;
It caused Jesus to leave heaven and come to earth;
It caused Jesus to lay down His life on the cross.

Sin is sin in the sight of God, no matter your excuse
It is an abomination in the sight of God
It will be punished sooner or later, dear friend,
It is full of deadly poison and toxins.

Sin requires forgiveness first from God,
It does require admitting it and confessing it,
It requires your complete round about turn to good;
It requires conscious effort to forsake it through the Holy Spirit.

Sin's forgiveness first is from the Almighty God,
It needs forgiveness from those affected by it,
It needs the sinner forgiving himself or herself;
It needs the blood of Jesus for complete cleansing.

Societal acceptance of that sin as a common norm,
Does not remove it from being sin in God's presence,
It does not remove its gravity or punishment,
Indeed the soul that sinneth will surely die.

Will you, dear friend, continue to toy with that sin?
Will you not remember that God is seeing it?
Will you stop refusing to admit this abomination?
Why not today do away with that sin completely?

© O.Ola- Ojo 1992

Grace or Works?

I Loved Them Both Dearly

*Mine were the two boys, both from my loins
the younger was somewhat lazy and inconsiderate
not too keen to work on the farms.
Selfish often in his thinking and actions
But, I loved him dearly.*

*Once he came to make a request of me
That of having his inheritance whilst I was alive
He couldn't wait for me to pass on to Glory
Selfishly he demanded his right at the wrong time
But I loved him still.*

*I gave him his inheritance and to a far country he went
Not telling me where he was off to and for how long
Not minding what torments his request had on us
To me, his mother, brother, family and friends
But I loved him nonetheless.*

*I was heartbroken when he left
I did not stop him travelling even though I could
I allowed him to go for a lifetime adventure
I believed and prayed he will come back home
For I loved him dearly.*

Poems

Everyday I watched out for his coming home
No one seemed to have a clue where he was
No one told me what sort of life he was living
No one but I kept on watching out for him
For I loved him still.

One ordinary day I saw someone coming up our path
Ragged, weary, worn out and in shame he came
Apologising for his past mistakes to God and to me
Asking that he be considered for a servant position
I loved him even more.

I embraced him in love and wept over him
Prayers answered and dreams come to pass
I ordered that he be clothed in new garments
A ring for his finger and shoes for his weary feet
And I loved him still.

I ordered that the fattened calf be killed
It was time for a huge family celebration
My younger son's return was worth it all
A time to publicly restore him to his sonship position
Now I loved him best.

My older son very obedient and hardworking
Unlike his brother never asking, hardly daring
Always by my side come rain come sunshine
He was on the farm when his younger brother arrived
I loved him very much too.

Grace or Works?

All these years he has worked by my side
Watching my character and attitude day and night
I longed for him to at least have an attitude like mine
Alas, he refused to come to the party because he was angry
But I loved him too.

I went out to meet him and asked why he was angry
He told me I had never given him a kid to celebrate with his friends
He judged his younger brother's lifestyle abroad without seeing him
He seemed to care less whether his younger brother lived or died.
But I loved him more.

All I have is yours son I told him to his amazement
You did not have because you did not ask me for anything
The blood of the calf has been shed in the party for you and your brother
The party is only for those who would come just as they were
I loved him too very much.

Mine were the two boys both from my loins
Different in character, attitude and traits
Same parents, same upbringing, same environment
Different in their thinking and life goals
But I loved them both dearly and equally too.

© O.Ola – Ojo 22/08/04 Luke 15: 11-32

Poems

God's Love Like the Sun

God's love to mankind is just like the sun
Constant in position, timing and size
Constant in intensity, never too hot or too cold
Bright enough to penetrate through the clouds.

Shining on the wicked and the upright indiscriminately
Reaching the poor and the rich no matter where
Enjoyable by the young and the old alike
Giving life and health to every living thing.

Immeasurable by any man or any scientific means
Can never be hidden by anything at anytime
Can never be covered, concealed or denied
Can always be received with childlike faith.

God's love has been given never to be withdrawn
We all live by His love which gives us life
Giving us enough strength and courage each day
Searching us out amongst our sins and hopelessness
Touching every part of our being, spiritual and physical.

Always available to every generation
Reaching the deepest sea and highest mountain
Melting every ice of uncertainty, doubt and loss
Banishing every darkness of despair and bondage
Releasing every ingredient for growth in every way
Bringing the best out of the worst of each sinner
Breaking every racial and social barrier.

©O.Ola – Ojo 18.05.1992

Grace or Works?

The Beauty of the Snow

Many children and adults like the time of snow every year
Despite the cold, it is a time for many activities and excitements
The snowball and snowman to make with friends and families
Sledging in the parks or on any available snow covered lands.

The power and the beauty of the snow cannot be imagined
It is better personally experienced than being told by anyone
The snow's uniqueness and beauty is worth waiting for
And need not be a barrier to the normal day-to-day activities.

The snow falls in tiny flakes evenly across the available open lands
Covering every house or shed roofs, open land and cars outside
In a matter of time everything uncovered outside gets covered
Houses, sheds, trees, cars, buses, roads all become white.

The snow's pure whiteness adds a distinctive colour and beauty
To every street, every road, every house and everything outside
It has the ability of covering everything evenly small or big
Nothing can stand in its way once the snow starts to fall whenever.

Poems

*The dirt on every road is well covered with no protruding part
Irrespective of any previous painting, all houses becomes white
Such is God's love capable of covering every sin from any man
That it becomes undetectable never again to Him once forgiven.*

*God's love is available to all mankind irrespective of their
background
It is evenly spread and constant in its ability and availability
As we expose our sins and weaknesses to His loving grace
He turns us spotless, faultless, unique and beautiful unto
Himself.*

*'Though your sins be as scarlet' God's promise to mankind
says
'Yet will I make them white as snow' the scripture tells us
'Though they be red as crimson'
'Yet will I make them white as wool'.*

*The period of snow for many is a matter of a season
Lasting between days and years in some artic part of the world
The beauty and the uniqueness can only be enjoyed so
long as it lasts
For then another season will soon be here according to
God's plans.*

Grace or Works?

The free gift of salvation dear friend is available now and free for all
For many the opportunity for salvation comes once,
for others many times
This is the day and time of salvation friend if you care to know
For once comes death after which comes God's judgement not mercy.

Will you today accept the gift of salvation with it's added benefits?
Experience the covering of your sins and past no matter how terrible
Enjoy the cooling fall and anointing power of the blessed Holy Spirit
Which today is falling everywhere, just like the beautiful snowflakes.

©O.Ola-Ojo 2/12/93. Isaiah 1:18-19

Summer In The West

Summer in the West is a period many people look forward to
The fields are green, the flowers blossom and the weather is warm
There are more variety in fruits, vegetables and foods that is available
It is a lovely time to work on the garden and sunbath.

Daily, many people listen to summer weather forecasts
Trips are planned and made to many continental countries
A very good time for many in the business world
Indeed a time to take a break from the routine, demanding jobs.

So much goes into planning summer holidays by many
From the visits to the travelling agencies, to the insurance companies
To direct enquiries from friends, family members and other associates
And for some, to the bank manager to get another 'summer loan'.

The privileged ones take a trip to yet another spot of their desire
Possibly in the company of a tour guide or alone by themselves

Grace or Works?

Taking many good 'snapshots' each day of their trip
To share with friends, family and close associates upon return.

Whilst the privileged treat themselves to good sunbath abroad
The under-privileged compensate for this by working in their gardens
Both get sun-tanned in the process so long as the weather is good
The excitement and experience shared sometimes for a long time to come.

Good as this is, yet sad is the ignorance of many
Little or no attention is paid to the summer of eternity
Paid for by Christ on the cross and prepared by God the Father
Insured by the Holy Spirit, a place of everlasting summer and eternity.

The weather forecast is clearly written in the Bible
Daily broadcast by anointed men of God through the media
Yet many fail to take this free offer of salvation and redemption
Whilst others procrastinate as if they have the control over their lives.

Beautiful as your garden may be this summer, dear friend
Exciting as your trip to the 'continent' may promise
None can be compared to the beauty, joy and excitement in heaven
Why will you refuse a healthy spiritual sunbath friend?

Grace or Works?

The earthly summer is periodic and very temporary
It offers sunbaths/tans that can only last for just a while
Promising as it may be, it is very much conditional
Each must make good use of it, or refuse and miss out

©O.Ola-Ojo 8/8/92

Grace or Works?

Cafeteria

Cafeterias provide food.
Various dishes for various times
Some are spicy; others are not
Some are sweet, others sour
Cold and hot drinks, snacks, sweets and fruits.

Some dishes take long to prepare and cook
Others a few minutes or perhaps seconds
Some dishes look really attractive and tempting
Other dishes simply look very plain and uninviting.

Some dishes are made for certain groups of people:
Vegetarians who don't eat any animal product,
The diabetics or some others on special diets,
Little children with taste buds often different from adults'.

Some dishes may not taste very nice but we eat them
To make us grow healthy and strong
Such are the lessons on faith, love and hope
Reflecting these in our lives makes us Christ like and useful.

Human beings have the tendency to be hungry for food.
As well as thirsty for a drink, cold or hot
Whilst some live to eat most of their lives
Others eat to live and face life's challenges.

At meal times the cafeteria trolleys are fully stocked
Some cafeterias have complete self-service
In others, orders are placed with the stewards.
In school cafeterias, there is minimal choice.

Grace or Works?

Stewards sometimes stand at the back of food trolleys
Watching customers and refilling the food trolleys,
Giving a helping hand in serving customers,
With someone at the cash till to be paid for the food taken.

The Bible is God's cafeteria for the world
With enough food for the hungry and drink for the thirsty
Every human spiritual need is already catered for,
Meeting every age group, ability and need.

The word of God is there at all times, in all seasons
The Psalms for encouragement, Proverbs for wisdom
Genesis for the creation story and revelations for the latter days
Matthew, Mark, Luke and John for Jesus' ministry
Ephesians, Corinthians, Colossians, Galatians
For rebuke and encouragement.

What then are you having friend at the next mealtime?
In the earthly cafeteria we pay for our choice,
In the Bible, God's cafeteria to mankind, Christ has paid
In full by His death on the cross
And by His stripes we are healed.

Heavenly hosts watch what we do at meal times
Christ on God's right hand always interceding on our behalf
Angels waiting upon us for our orders in God
How often do you visit God's cafeteria for mankind?

Jeremiah 31:25. © O.Ola- Ojo 20/04/96

Grace or Works?

MY PERSONAL NOTES

Opportunity To Become A Christian

Dear Father in heaven,
Thank you for the privilege of reading this book. 'Indeed I have sinned and come short of Your glory.' I am grateful to You for sending Jesus Christ into this world to come to die on the cross of Calvary for me. I believe in my heart that Jesus Christ paid for my sins, past, present and future. I believe Jesus Christ was buried and on the third day He rose from the dead. I believe that Jesus Christ will come back again. I confess with my mouth and I accept Him now to be my Lord.
Master, Saviour, Brother, and Friend. I ask in Your mercy for the infilling of theHoly Spirit so that with His help, I can live a victorious life becoming all that You have ordained me to be in Jesus' name. I pray with thanksgiving. Amen.

If after reading this book you said the above prayer and became born-again, 'Congratulations! You are Born Again' is a booklet for those who have done so through reading this book. It is a free booklet that we would like you to have. In it, the frequently asked questions are answered and this will get you on the way to growing in your newfound faith in God. You can download this free booklet from our website: www.protokospublishers.com

You may also contact any of the organisations listed at the end of the book.

I look forward to hearing from you soon.
O. Ola –Ojo (2009)

Aglow International
Web site: www.aglow.org
Aglow International is a network of caring women, a faith-building organisation rooted in local groups and international in scope, yet one-on-one in ministry. Their mission is to lead women to Jesus Christ and provide opportunity for Christian women to grow in their faith and minister to others.

Care for the Family
PO Box 488
Cardiff
CF15 7YY
Tel: (029) 2081 0800
Fax: (029) 2081 4089
Email: mail@cff.org.uk
Web site: www.care-for-the-family.org.uk OR www.cff.org.uk
Care for the Family aims to promote strong family life and to help those hurting because of family breakdown. Their heart is to come alongside people in the good times and in the tough times – bringing hope, compassion and some practical, down-to-earth help and encouragement.

Children Evangelism Ministry Inc
P.O. Box 4480
Ilorin, Kwara State,
Nigeria.
Tel: +234 31 222199
E-mail: cem@ilorin.skannet.com OR cem562000@yahoo.com
Children Evangelism Ministry Inc is a ministry that reaches out with the Gospel to children before and after birth. The ministry teaches and equips parents, teachers and co-ordinators of Sunday Schools and Children's Clubs. They also have and hold Children's Clubs, conferences and training seminars.

Focus on the Family
Tel: 1-800 - 232 6459
Web site: www.family.org
Focus on the Family cooperates with the Holy Spirit in disseminating the Gospel of Jesus Christ to as many people as possible, and, specifically, to accomplish that objective by helping to preserve traditional values and the institution of the family.

Full Gospel Business Men's Fellowship
http://www.fgbmfi.org/who.htm
Full Gospel Business Men's Fellowship –They reach men in all nations for Jesus Christ, calling men back to God. They help believers to be baptized in the Holy Spirit and to grow spiritually. They train and equip men to fulfil the Great Commission. They provide an opportunity for Christian fellowship and bring greater unity among all people in the body of Christ.

Mike Barber Ministries
http://www.mikebarber.org/main/ - They are dedicated to reaching men and women prisoners with the love of Jesus Christ and word of God.

Open Gate
DR2 DV8
2 Union Road
Croydon
CR0 2XU.
Tel: 0208 665 5533
Fax: 0208 684 7233
e-mail: opengate@yahoo.co.uk
      alteschool@yahoo.co.uk
Open Gate Provides a preventative and supplementary

educational facility for youths at risk of permanent exclusion. They aim at empowering and connecting the youths for the future. They provide support for the family and the community.

Prodigals Only
www.prodigalsonly.com - This site is for prodigals who are sick and tired of being a prodigal and would want to come back home to the Loving arms of God.

Protokos Publishers
www.protokospublishers.com - This site provides various resources for the family.

The Shepherd's Ministries
5 Brookehowse Road
Bellingham
London SE6 3TJ, UK
Tel/Fax: +44 208 698 7222
Email: info@theshepherdsministries.org
Web site: www.theshepherdsministries.org
The Shepherd's Ministries helps to bring children into an experience of worshipping God in truth and in spirit; give children a world-view based on God's word and mission and helps children to exercise their gifts in local and global missions.

Teenagers' Outreach Ministries (TOM) Inc.
Plot 85
Ladi Kwali Ext. Layout,
P.O.Box 16
Kwali,Abuja.
Nigeria.
Tel- 02082933730

Fax-02082933731
Nigeria - 08037044195
- 07081860407
Email- tominthq@yahoo.co.uk
Web site -www.tominternational .org
The Teenagers' Outreach Ministries (TOM) Inc. has a vision of leading today's teenager to Christ. This forms the foundation on which we mould their character in line with the word of God, thereby equipping them to fulfil their God ordained roles in life.

Total Woman Ministries
3 Herringham Road
Thames Wharf Barrier,
Charlton,
London
SE7 8NJ.
Tel: 020 8293 3730
Fax: 020 8293 3731
Email: admin@totalwomanministries.org
Web site:www.totalwomanministries.org
Total Woman Ministries by God's grace has the sole vision of reaching out to women of all categories (married, single, separated / divorced, young, middle-aged or elderly).

OTHER BOOKS BY THE AUTHOR:

Provocation, Prayer and Praise
(December 2004 & 2009)

Complimentary to The Christian and Infertility this book focuses on the story of an infertile woman in the Bible, her provocations, prayer and praise. Whatever makes you incomplete, unfulfilled, less than whom God made you to be, whatever issue of life that the enemy uses to provoke you calls for prayer.

Key features include:
- Some known medical reasons for infertility in the women.
- Why Hannah went to the house of God in spite of her barrenness.
- Is it true that the husband is much more than 10 sons to the infertile woman?
- When, where and how to address the source/cause of your provocation.
- God's part and your part in that promise.
- God is able to met that humanly impossible need of yours.
- A time to celebrate and praise God.

Book Details:
Paperback: 128 pages
Language English
ISBN-13: 978-0-9557898-3-0

A Reader from London, 7 Jan 2006 on Amazon.co.uk
An excellent easy to read and understand book. The principles shared in this book though primarily are for those trying for a baby could as well be applied to any area of hurt and un-fulfilment.

 :www.protokospublishers.com

Grace or Works?

The Christian and Infertility
(December 2004 & 2009)

The Christian and Infertility addresses one of the often neglected needs of Christian couples. It gives an insight into infertility from the biblical and medical perspectives. It is written not only for potential fruitful couples but for pastors, family and friends of these couples. It is written that the Body of Christ might be fully equipped to know and support couples who are facing the challenge of infertility at present.

Key features include:
- Childleness in the Bible and lessons to learn;
- Some possible physical, medical and environmental causes of infertility;
- Some known spiritual causes of infertility;
- The man and low sperm count;
- Some of the available treatment optons in the UK;
- Choice of fertility treatment;
- Should a christian professional be involved in fertility treatment?

Book Details:
Paperback: 146 pages
Language English
ISBN-13: 978-0-9557898-2-3

A reviewer from Glen Burnie, USA, 29 Oct 2007 on Amazon.co.uk'
The book is a great eye-opener for all. It sheds light on infertility from the medical and spiritual angle. This gives the reader a balance because i believe every human being is made up of both physical and spiritual part. To get a balance in life, the two parts must be well fed. One must not concentrate on the spiritual and neglect the physical part. The book also reminds us that God has a way of sorting us out.... The book is quite inspiring. I will recommend this book to everybody trusting God for any form of blessing from God to go get one and apply it to his or her situation. It will definitely bless you and yours'.

 :www.protokospublishers.com

Obstetrics and Gynaecology Ultrasound - A Self-Assessment Guide

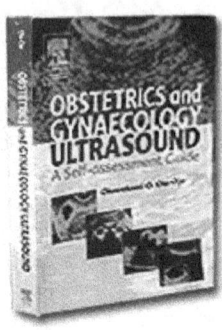

June 2005 Churchill Elsevier Publishers, UK.

This self-assessment guide is a structured questions and answer book that develops the reader's understanding capability using a simple method in treating related topics. Clinical indications are presented with their corresponding ultrasound findings using appropriate illustrations. A case study approach is followed; presenting the clinical and ethical dilemmas that might arise whilst encouraging students to think. The aim is to reinforce theoretical knowledge within a clinical environment.

Key features:
- Over 600 high-resolution ultrasound images
- Cover a wide spectrum of ultrasound curriculum.
- Includes a detailed study of fertility.
- Aids quick understanding of subject matter.
- 468 pages.

ISBN-10: 0443064628
ISBN-13: 978-0443064623
Book Dimensions: 24 x 16.8 x 2.6 cm

"...*This excellent new book is a study guide... This is an attractive paperback that should be essential reading for trainee obstetric and gynaecological sonographers, whether they are radiographers or radiology or obstetric trainees. It will be of particular value to those preparing for the RCOG/RCR Diploma in Advanced Obstetric Ultrasound and to specialist registrars in obstetrics and gynaecology undertaking special skills modules in fetal medicine, gynaecological ultrasound and infertility...*"

The Obstetrician & Gynaecologist, www.rcog.org.uk/togonline
Book reviews 2006

Reviewer **Ann Harper MD FRCPI FRCOG.**
Consultant Obstetrician and Gynaecologist
Royal Jubilee Maternity Service, Belfast., UK

 :www.protokospublishers.com

Grace or Works?

GOOD MUMS, BAD MUMS
(June 2005 & 2009)

This is in two parts, the main chapter that can be used for personal or group study, and an accompanying exercise section. The privileged position of a mother is in her being a co-creator with God and bringing forth life (lives). This book compliments one of God's previous revelations to me as contained in the book titled Good Dads, Bad Dads'. Whilst the father could be likened to the pilot of the family plane, the mother can be likened to the force behind the plane – positive or negative. Good mothers are not only co-creators with God, they also do nurture as well as nourish their children physically, emotionally and spiritually.

Keys Features:
- Were all the mothers in the Bible god mothers?
- Lessons from the strengths and weakness of seven mothers.
- Be encouraged - you are not alone in the assignment of motherhood.
- Be motivated in the areas of your strengths.
- Learn ways of supporting your husband and children.

Book Details:
Paperback: 162 pages
Language English
ISBN-13: 978-0-9557898-1-6
Book Dimensions: 21.4 x 14 x 1.4 cm

 :www.protokospublishers.com

Grace or Works?

To the Bride with Love
(2007 & 2009)

Every wise woman preparing to get married knows she will need sound advice, practical tips and solid, heartfelt prayers, of those who have travelled on the road she is about to journey on. In this book, 10 women of different age groups, from different backgrounds and cultures who wedded under various circumstances, individually share their experience with the bride in an intimate, very candid and unforgettable way.

Book details:
Paperback: 108 pages
Language English
ISBN-13: 978-0-9557898-4-7
Book Dimensions: 22.4 x 15 x 1 cm

To the Bride with Love is the perfect bride's evergreen companion. The content is suitable, relevant and applicable even decades after the wedding day.
To the Bride with Love is an ideal wedding gift on its own. It can also accompany any other gift (big or small) that you have for the bride but take this hint... the bride will keep thanking you for the book years and years after.

'One of the best', 19 Jul 2008 on Amazon.com
Sade Olaoye "clare4good" (United Kingdom)
This book has really helped my marriage from the onset as I got it as a wedding gift, God bless the giver. It's a must read fro relationship improvement and God's guidance. I recommend people to get for oneself and also as a great blessing for someone else in love. "To the Bride with Love"

Review by Oyinlola Odunlami CEO.
Shallom Bookshop, London UK

The writing style of Oluwakemi is unique, peculiar and distinct to herself. I recommend To the Bride with Love to wives, wives to be, mothers, mentors, youth leaders and workers. Why? The clarity, the focus and the intent of this book is so empowering, encouraging and enlightening that it will definitely mould or re mould a life to achieve its purpose. The truth is, there are very few books that have depth as well as help you to achieve your goals and arrive at your destination. Many books tend to excite you but have no depth; you read and you forget; they do not really change you but this book, To the Bride with Love will definitely leave a word in your spirit and move you to your next level!

I believe that this is also a book that pastors will find useful as a manual for marriage counselling, because many books on marriage focus mostly on what you as an individual can gain, your own personal satisfaction while little is said about the sacrifices involved and their importance. As my pastor usually says, it is important to learn from those who have gone ahead, understand why some were successful and others weren't, so that we won't fall where they fell, rather, we would gain more speed, achieve our goals and thereby glorify Christ.

So, I invite you not only to get a copy of this life-changing manual for yourself, but also to put it into as many hands as you can afford to, for then the world will definitely benefit and your life will be a blessing to many.

 :www.protokospublishers.com

Refuge Under His Wings

"*an exhaustive analysis of the Book of Ruth in the Bible. The author combines her deep Christian conviction and excellent knowledge of the Holy Scriptures to produce a must read for every Christian, married or single. The book is interspaced with beautifully written prayers, which enables the reader to pause, pray and meditate on the revelations received... The book is also loaded with poetry like 'Thy will be done oh Lord' for those who may be facing an uncertain future or on a cross road of decisions.*"

Dr E B Ekpo MD, FRCP
Queen Elizabeth Hospital, Christian Fellowship,
Woolwich, London. UK

"...[a] ...spiritually sound book... a fine work of thoughtful reading and study... I therefore recommend it to every Christian, married or single....
Pat Roach Senior Pastor
New Covenant Church.
Wandsworth Branch, London. UK.

Book details:
Paperback: 100 pages
Language English
ISBN-10: 095578980X
ISBN-13: 978-0955789809

This book feeds the soul. Most of all I loved the poetry. It gives you time to savour the thoughts as reader. There is a good mix of poetry and prose. To look at the story of Ruth in depth gave good spiritual food. You can pause and take it in at your own pace. The meditation on Psalm 121 was good also. There's nothing like reading a Psalm slowly and meditating on its contents. The author's own reflections allow you to see the book through someone else's eyes. A good read.

Book Review: by **Gaby Richards**, London, UK.

 :www.protokospublishers.com

COMING OUT SOON

- Good Dads, Bad Dads.

- Let's Reason Together - Youth's A-Z.

Dear Reader,

Thank you for your time and resources committed to supporting this writing ministry. Please help to tell others about how much the Lord has blessed you reading this book.

You will certainly be blessed by the other books written by Oluwakemi, so why not visit www.protokospublishers.com and place an order today.

It will equally be appreciated if you can help to write a few sentences review of the book on www.amazon.com and / or on www.protokospublishers.com.

Please note that all our books are easily available from our website.

God bless you as you do.
Management
Protokos Publishers.

www.ingramcontent.com/pod-product-compliance
Lightning Source LLC
Chambersburg PA
CBHW051452290426
44109CB00016B/1719